THE FARBERWARE®
WORLD OF WOK
COOKERY

BY
GAIL PIAZZA

DORISON HOUSE PUBLISHERS
BOSTON

About the Author

Gail Piazza is a Home Economics Consultant who received her B. A. degree in Foods and Nutrition from College Miserecordia in Dallas, Pennsylvania. She earned her Master's degree from the New York University School of Education.

As a specialist in product and recipe testing and development, she has worked on many promotional cookbooks and use and care manuals for companies such as Farberware, and assisted another cookbook author with several books.

In addition, Gail works as a food stylist. She has prepared food for photography for major movie productions, television commercials, and the cover of this cookbook.

Her husband and children, with whom she lives in Washingtonville, New York, enjoy Gail's cooking, and especially loved these foods from the wok. We're sure you will, too!

Acknowledgments

My thanks to the following people at Farberware for the opportunity to write this book and for their encouragement and assistance:

Kathy Cripps
  Director, Product Information Center
Amy Christensen
  Senior Home Economist

To Barbara Weinand, a thank you for helping me to test many of the recipes in this book.

An extra special thanks to my husband Jerry for his unending help and encouragement. Without him this book would never have been written.

Gail Piazza
Author

Copyright

Contents

Introduction: Why a wok?

Your wok is the single most important cooking utensil used in oriental cooking. It is ideally suited to the ancient method of Chinese cooking, called "stir-frying." In addition to its well-known talent for stir-frying, it excells at deep-frying, shallow-frying, steaming, and simmering.

As you master the art of oriental cooking, you will be learning many new oriental cooking techniques. Steaming and red or white stewing are major types of cooking employed by the Chinese. You will find that when using a steamer insert or rack with the dome-shaped stainless steel cover of your wok, moisture is kept inside to continuously baste the food, keeping it moist, tender and juicy.

The wok is a remarkably versatile appliance. For instance, it is a perfect donut maker. Because of its shape there is a large surface area of oil in comparison to an ordinary deep-fryer. This means much less oil is needed to make the same number of donuts at one time. The donuts turn out light and greaseless because the heat is controlled at just the right level. Obviously then, it is also an excellent deep-fryer for every other food cooked in that manner.

You can also use your wok to make candy — something that many people hesitate to cook because it requires accurate temperature control and the pan can be difficult to clean. There are several candy recipes in this book that are simple and do not require the use of a candy thermometer. Best of all the cleanup is a snap. After you have finished your candy making, fill the wok with water and bring it to a rolling boil. This will loosen the sticky residue leaving virtually no further work. The cleanup is complete.

The wok is perfect as an omelet pan and if you follow the instructions in this book you will get beautiful results every time. And crêpes can be made perfectly in the wok.

You'll want to use the electric wok as a buffet server. It will keep your foods nicely warm so that all your guests are served food at the proper temperature, regardless of when they get to the table.

Since the electric wok can easily be used right at the dinner table it can be used as a fondue pot.

World of Wok Cookery covers cooking as well as preparation techniques, including the use of the cooking chopsticks which come with your Farberware Wok Set. A glossary of oriental ingredients is included to give you a brief description of some foods you may not be familiar with.

Organization is the most important word to keep in mind in order to create a successful oriental meal. Until you feel comfortable with oriental cooking you may wish to consult the menu planning and serving chapter for help in arranging and preparing your meals.

A country's cuisine is affected by its climate and culture; we will touch on the characteristics of several of China's provinces as well as Japan, Korea, India and the Hawaiian Islands for a brief look at the people, their food and its preparation.

Many oriental recipes, some very foreign to the American palate, will be presented in the eastern section of this book. In the western section of the book you are sure to find more familiar dishes.

Each recipe in this book has been specifically developed for use in the Farberware Stainless Steel Wok. Every one was kitchen-tested with the American "oriental cook" in mind.

Explore these pages and discover the many new and different ways to enjoy your wok. It's unsurpassable for nutritious, economical food preparation. We know you will find wok cooking to be rewarding while opening up a whole new world of taste delights for you and your family.

Traditional Cooking Methods

In order to be a practiced oriental cook these are the cooking and cutting techinques you should learn:

Stir-frying — *Chao*

Stir-frying is the most uniquely oriental of all the traditional cooking methods. It is simply the rapid cooking of uniformly cut pieces of meat and vegetables in a small amount of hot oil over high heat. It is a type of "flash cooking" in which you constantly toss the food. There are a few important principles to learn if you are to get the best results. They will be found on page 17 in the section titled How to Stir-fry.

Shallow-frying — *Chien*

Shallow-frying is a traditional oriental technique in which about one half cup of vegetable oil is heated over medium heat. Heat oil in the wok placed on the ring over the burner or heating element; or set the heat control dial to 350° F. and wait until the light goes out. Add food and brown on one side and then the other, turning once or twice until nicely browned. This method is used mainly for browning meats to seal in the natural juices.

Deep-frying — *Tsa*

When deep-frying, two to four cups of oil are heated over high heat. Place the wok on the ring over the burner or heating element. Add oil and heat until it is very hot, about 375° F., for five to eight minutes. When using the electric wok be sure the surface it is on is clean, dry and level. Add oil and set the heat control dial to 425° F. When the oil has reached the proper temperature the light will go out. Carefully place food a few pieces at a time into the wok, frying until golden brown, turning as needed. Drain on the tempura rack or absorbent paper towels and then after allowing the oil to come back up to temperature, repeat the process until all the food is fried.

Stewing — *Shoa*

Stewing is the cooking of meats in a large amount of liquid for a long period of time, generally from one to five hours. This is done at a low temperature. This type of cooking is used to tenderize tough cuts of meat. There are two classifications of stewing, red and white. Red stewing is so called because soy sauce is used as the stewing liquid. In white stewing a light broth or water is used.

Steaming — *Cheng*

Steaming is a very popular method of cooking both here and in the orient. It is a very satisfactory way to prepare meats, fish, vegetables and desserts. Flavor is locked in, color is heightened and vitamins and minerals are retained in the cooking liquid. In this method, the food is placed on a steaming insert or rack. If you don't have either of these use a round cake cooling rack or a metal pie plate filled with holes. The rack is placed above a small amount of boiling water. All steaming is done with the cover on. Cooking time will depend on sizes of pieces and types of food. For best texture and results, have food to be steamed at room temperature.

Chinese Cooking Tools

To make a recipe as authentic as possible the ingredients must be prepared in precisely the right manner. To do this a few basic tools are necessary.

Wok

As you know, the most important tool is the wok. However, you may not be aware of ways to use it to its fullest potential. This versatile piece can be used to prepare a wide range of foods, from omelets to candy.

If you own an electric wok, use it to cook directly at the table or use it as a buffet server. The next time you are having company to dinner, prepare the ingredients for a stir-fried recipe the night before or early in the day. Put them in attractive small bowls and place them on a serving tray. When it is time to eat bring the prepared tray and electric wok to the table. Join your guests and prepare dinner right at the table. Serve and keep any extra portions warm for second helpings. Everyone will enjoy the meal, especially you.

Your wok becomes a steamer with the addition of a steamer insert which is a round perforated metal plate designed to fit in the wok. Stackable chinese bamboo steamers are also designed to fit into the wok. To steam, you place a small amount of boiling water on the bottom of the wok. Add the steamer insert and then the food. Cover and steam according to recipe directions.

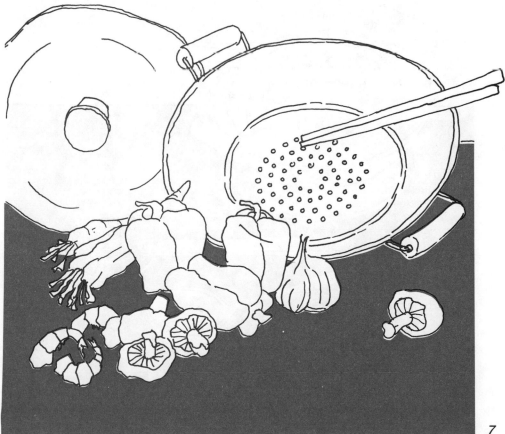

7

Utensils

There are a few cooking utensils that are traditional companions to the wok. The long handled spoon or ladle, the long handled spatula, which has a wide curved edge and resembles a shovel, and the cooking chopsticks are all used in stir-frying to toss and turn the food. The ladle may be used to transfer oil or broth from a pot or nearby container as needed while you are stir-frying. It may also be used to remove prepared food from the wok to free it for additional stir-frying. If you do not have these items, you can use standard long handled metal kitchen spatulas and ladles.

Tempura rack

When you are deep-frying you will find the tempura rack a very handy accessory. The semi-circular wire draining rack attaches to the side of the wok. You place the finished fried foods on the rack where they drain and keep warm while other foods are being fried.

Wire skimmer

The wire skimmer is also especially useful when deep-frying to remove finished food. The excess oil drains through the wire mesh back into the wok. As you are deep-frying bits of batter and food will accumulate. Use the wire skimmer to remove them and keep the oil clean. If they are not removed they will burn and cause smoking.

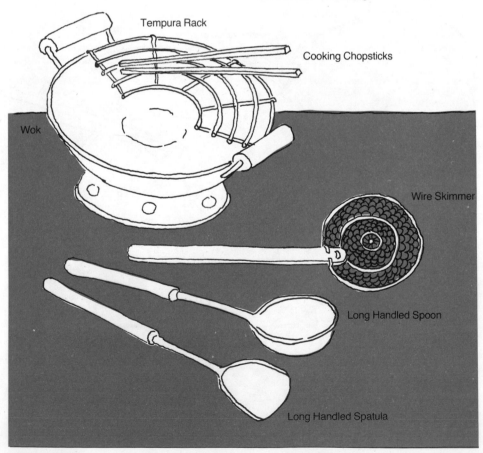

Tempura Rack

Cooking Chopsticks

Wok

Wire Skimmer

Long Handled Spoon

Long Handled Spatula

Cleaver

Most oriental recipes call for cutting, slicing, dicing, shredding or mincing. In China, the cleaver is the chef's most valuable tool for cutting. They come in several weights. The blades can be carbon or stainless steel. This tool can be used for all the cutting tasks you will encounter. If you are intimidated by this tool, a large very sharp knife will suffice. Whichever you choose, remember that for best results you should always keep the blade sharp.

Food processor

This is the newest and most versatile aid for the cutting, chopping, shredding and pureeing chores. You can do in minutes what would otherwise take hours. If you own a food processor you will use it often when preparing oriental recipes. Follow the directions for slicing, chopping and pureeing that you will find in the use and care manual packaged with the machine. Note that when slicing meat either with the food processor or by hand, it is much easier if it is partially frozen. You will get more uniform and thinner slices.

Cutting board

Invest in a good thick cutting board that is large enough to hold a good amount of food. Keep it clean by washing often with a nylon sponge, and occasionally rubbing it down with salt and lemon.

Having the necessary tools and using them correctly will make your oriental food preparation easy and rewarding.

Timers

Many of these recipes call for cooking food for less than 5 minutes. An egg timer or a stop watch would be useful in those cases.

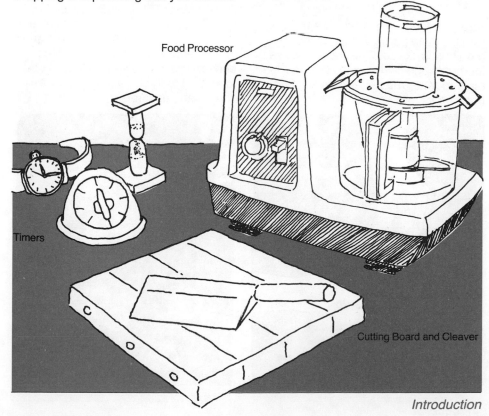

Food Processor

Timers

Cutting Board and Cleaver

Cutting Techniques

Slicing, roll-slicing, shredding, dicing, chopping, mincing and pureeing are the basic cutting techniques to master for the proper preparation of oriental dishes.

The size, shape and texture of the individual food items in a recipe will dictate which techniques to employ.

Oriental cooks take great pride in the appearance as well as the flavor of the food they serve. In addition to providing a more pleasing appearance, ingredients are cut to a uniform size and shape in order to insure similar cooking times. If meats are cubed, sliced or shredded, then the vegetables are cut the same way. The cooking time is decreased by increasing the amount of surface area exposed to the heat. Smaller pieces also allow for more absorption of the sauce, giving a better flavor.

Slicing

Straight: Cutting is done straight down with the knife perpendicular to the ingredient as it is cut. This method is used for meats and fleshy vegetables like mushrooms, water chestnuts and bamboo shoots.

Diagonal or Angle-slicing: The knife is held on a slant and the food is cut diagonally. Celery, carrots, asparagus, Chinese cabbage and other stringy stalky vegetables as well as flank steak are cut this way. In addition to being attractive, more of the food's surface is exposed to the heat, reducing cooking time.

Roll-slicing: This is similar to angle-slicing. The knife is held on a slant but after each cut the vegetable is turned a quarter turn and sliced at an angle in the opposite direction. This method is used for cutting tough fibrous vegetables like carrots and asparagus.

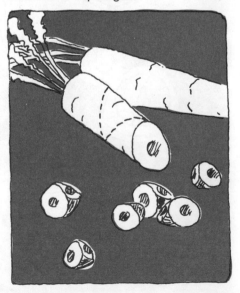

Shredding

Food is cut in thin julienne-type strips. First you straight-cut the meat or vegetable into thin slices and then you stack the slices one on top of the other and slice again into matchstick pieces. For best results when you are shredding, hold the top of the knife down on the board and lift only the back to slice.

Mincing

This is done in the same manner as chopping except that you continue to work the knife until the food is cut into the smallest possible pieces.

Dicing

Food is cut into lengthwise strips and then the strips are cut into ⅛ to ⅜-inch uniform squares.

Chopping

Food is cut into small slices, or wedges. Then, holding the point of the knife down you raise and lower the back of the blade, cutting the food into smaller uniform pieces.

Pureeing

Food is reduced to a semi-liquid state. No pieces are visible. To puree, a blender, food mill or food processor must be used.

11

Before you cook remember!

A checklist of important things to remember before you begin to cook.

1. Take time to learn the basic cooking and cutting techniques.

2. Have all ingredients prepared and assembled before you do any cooking.

3. Do not overcook. Always use fresh or frozen vegetables. Most canned vegetables with the exception of canned oriental vegetables, are too soft for this type of cooking. Vegetables are always served crisp.

4. Always use peanut oil or other vegetable oils. They have a higher smoking point and allow higher temperatures to be used. The hotter the oil the less it is absorbed by the food.

5. When planning a menu for a complete oriental meal choose from several of the cooking categories. Check the menu planning section in this book for ideas. Don't pick more than two stir-fried dishes. They require last minute cooking and things will get too hectic. One stewed item and one steamed dish along with the stir-fry will be a good choice.

6. Don't forget that your electric wok can go directly to the table for guest participation and cooking or buffet serving. Check the Specialties and Banquet section for ideas.

7. Make up your own recipes. Check the charts in How to Create an Oriental Recipe of Your Own (pages 17-19) for help.

8. Convert a standard wok recipe to electric wok cooking by checking the conversion chart on page 19.

9. Be sure to wait until the light goes out on the electric wok before adding next ingredients. The wok is at the correct temperature only when light is out.

Menu Planning and Serving

When planning an oriental dinner party, you must, as in any other type of party do most of the preparation ahead of time. There are many soups, steamed, stewed and deep-fried dishes that can be prepared entirely ahead of time and be very successfully reheated in your oven or wok.

In China, when guests are coming to dinner, the number of foods prepared depends on the number of guests. One dish is prepared for each person. There are small amounts of many items as in a smorgasbord or buffet.

The following menus have been designed to allow you to spend as much time as possible with your guests. They avoid foods which require a good deal of preparation just prior to serving.

Use these sample menus as guides for planning your own party.

Remember to choose from several cooking categories and try to avoid too many of similarly flavored foods. These flavor categories include salty, sweet, sour, pungent, spicy and bitter.

Dim Sum
An Oriental Style Brunch

Hors d'oeuvres:

Steamed Stuffed Mushrooms (page 76)

Deep-fried Shrimp and Rice Balls (page 50)   Egg Rolls (page 38)

Deep-fried Spareribs (page 35)

Mustard Sauce (page 23)   Plum Sauce (page 22)

Sweet and Sour Sauce (page 23)

Main course:

Chicken with Red Wine Sediment Paste (page 54)

Twice-cooked Pork Szechuan (page 62)

Dessert:

Deep-fried Lemon Drop Cakes (page 52)   Pineapple Chunks

Fortune Cookies

Tea

Time Schedule For Dim Sum:

Early in the day: Cook all items except mushrooms. Prepare mushrooms up to cooking and refrigerate.

15 minutes before serving: Steam mushrooms according to recipe instructions.

Reheat: Deep-fried Shrimp and Rice, Egg Rolls, Deep-fried Spareribs, Chicken with Red Wine Sediment Paste and Twice-cooked Pork Szechuan.

Serve all items together as a buffet. Traditionally, each item is eaten from a separate dish but this is not necessary.

Oriental Dinner for 4-6 People

Hors d'oeuvres:

Peppery Meatballs with Mustard Sauce (page 65)   Fried Wontons (page 40)

Soup:

Egg Drop Soup (page 43)

First course:

Deep-fried Spareribs (page 35)
Sweet and Sour Sauce (page 23)   Plum Sauce (page 22)

Main course:

Brown Noodle Pancake with Chicken and Snow Peas (page 27)
Beef with Snow Peas, Tomatoes and Onions (page 34)

Dessert

Korean Cinnamon Cakes (page 92)

Time Schedule for Dinner for 4-6 People:

Early in the day: Cook: Peppery Meatballs with Mustard Sauce, Fried Wontons, Egg Drop Soup, Deep-fried Spareribs and Korean Cinnamon Cakes. Prepare: ingredients for Brown Noodle Pancake with Chicken and Snow Peas and Beef with Onions, Tomatoes and Snow Peas.

30 minutes before dinner: Reheat Hors d'oeuvres and serve.

15 minutes before dinner: Cook: Brown Noodle Pancake with Chicken and Snow Peas. Reheat soup. At the dinner table prepare: Beef with Onions, Tomatoes and Snow Peas.

Guest Participation Dinner

Tempura (page 84)
or
Peking Precious Pot (page 31)

Time Schedule for Guest Participation Dinner:

Early in the day: Prepare all ingredients for recipes. Place ingredients in an attractive tray for table preparation. Follow recipe instructions.

Oriental Buffet for 8-10 People

Hors d'oeuvres:

Chicken-filled Dumplings (page 77)   Fried Wontons (page 40)
Braised Spareribs (page 66)
Mustard Sauce (page 23)   Plum Sauce (page 22)
Sweet and Sour Sauce (page 23)

Main Course:

Steamed Chicken with Ham and Broccoli (page 50)
Savory Leg of Lamb (page 56)   Szechuan Shrimp (page 64)

Dessert:

Apricot-filled Deep-fried Cakes (page 48)
Glazed Bananas and Coconut Fritters (page 99)

Tea

Time Schedule for Oriental Buffet for 8-10 People:

Early in the day: Prepare all Hors d'oeuvres, Savory Leg of Lamb, and all ingredients for Steamed Chicken and Szechuan Shrimp

45 minutes before dinner: Reheat Hors d'oeuvres in 350° F. oven for 10 to 15 minutes. Serve with sauces while you prepare last minute items.*

30 minutes before dinner: Prepare Steamed Chicken. Keep warm in 150° F. oven.

Immediately before dinner: Prepare Szechuan Shrimp.

* *Always keep a supply of Mustard Sauce, Plum Sauce and Sweet and Sour Sauce in your refrigerator. They can be used for any hors d'oeuvre as a dipping sauce.*

How to create an oriental recipe of your own

You can make an oriental stir-fried dish of your very own with a little bit of imagination and ordinary ingredients found in your refrigerator, home garden or cupboard. Follow the stir-frying instructions, consult the stir-frying timing chart and choose one of the basic sauce recipes (see pages 22 and 23), and you will have made a delicious quick, nutritious recipe of your own.

How to stir-fry

1. The cardinal rule is **Be Prepared.** Have all ingredients cut and assembled before cooking. Marinate meat if desired in sauce mixture described below while you prepare remaining ingredients.

2. Always start with a clean dry wok. Pour 2 tablespoons of oil into the wok. Heat the wok on the heating element or burner and wait for oil to ripple or set heat control dial at 350° F. and wait until light goes out.

3. Stir-fry each ingredient separately as some vegetables take longer than others. Consult the timing chart. For best results cook in small batches. Add additional oil after each ingredient or as needed. Heat and continue as above. Push finished ingredients up the sides of the wok or remove if space does not permit.

4. Stir-fry garlic, nuts and pork first then do firmer vegetables, beef, chicken, seafood, and finally softer vegetables. Do not overcook. All vegetables should be crisp.

5. Combine sauce ingredients (see pages 22 and 23). Always stir cornstarch into cold liquid until smooth before adding to the wok.

6. Add sauce to the vegetables.

7. Return all stir-fried vegetables to the wok.

8. Toss to coat each piece. Reheat for 1 to 2 minutes or until liquid thickens and vegetables are hot. Do not overcook. Serve immediately.

One pound of meat, poultry or fish and one pound of vegetables will serve four to six people.

Fresh vegetables are best for stir-frying because vegetables should be served crisp, something which cannot be done with canned ingredients. You can grow your own oriental vegetables for a fraction of the cost of buying them. Growing your own supply also eliminates having to hunt for fresh or uncommon items. Many mail order seed catalogues carry a full line of oriental vegetable seeds.

Stir-fry Timing Guide

Food	Cutting Instructions	Stir-fry Time
Nuts Peanuts, cashews walnuts	Whole	1-2 minutes
Meats		
Pork	Thin strips	2 minutes
	1-inch chunks	3-5 minutes
	ground	1-2 minutes
	thin shreds	1 minute
Chicken	strips	2-3 minutes
	chunks	3-5 minutes
	shreds	1-2 minutes
Beef	angle-cut thin straight thin strips slices	2-3 minutes
Shrimp	whole	3 minutes
Vegetables		
Bamboo shoots	sliced	1 minute
Bean sprouts	whole	1 minute
Bok Choy	1-inch pieces	2 minutes
Broccoli	separated into smallest florets stems cut in ¼-inch pieces	3-5 minutes
Carrots	angle-cut in ¼-inch slices	2-3 minutes
	roll-cut in small pieces	3-5 minutes
Cauliflower	separated into small florets and cut in ½-inch pieces	3-5 minutes
Celery	angle-cut in ¼-inch slices	2-3 minutes
Chinese cabbage	1-inch pieces	1-2 minutes
	chopped	1 minute
Garlic	whole, mashed (to discard)	1 minute
	minced	30 seconds
Ginger root	cut ¼-inch thick (to discard)	1 minute
Green beans	angle-cut in ¼-inch pieces	3-5 minutes
Green peppers	thin strips	2 minutes
	1-inch cubes	2 minutes
Mushrooms	¼-inch slices	2 minutes
Onions	shreds	2 minutes
	wedges	2-3 minutes
Scallions	sliced	1-2 minutes
	chopped	30 seconds
Water chestnuts	sliced	1-2 minutes
Zucchini	¼-inch slices	1-2 minutes

How to grow bean sprouts

Bean sprouts are a very common oriental ingredient and you do not need a garden or even a light to grow them. Most seed catalogues as well as many health food stores carry the mung bean, the most commonly used bean for sprouting. To grow them place 3 table-spoons of beans in a quart-sized jar. Cover the beans with about 2 cups of water and soak over night. Drain the water and cover the jar with cheesecloth held in place with a rubber band. Put the covered jar in a clean, dark dry place. Rinse the beans three times a day by draining the water through the cheesecloth and adding fresh water. The sprouts will be ready for use in three to five days. Rinse them well and use in stir-fried dishes, omelets and salads. Leftover sprouts can be stored in a covered container for a day or two.

How to convert a recipe to electric wok cooking

If you have a recipe that calls for cooking in a wok, steamer, fry pan or deep-fryer and you want to use your electric wok, the following chart will give proper temperature settings for conversion to electric cooking.

Cooking method	Non-electric instruction	Electric temperature
Stir-frying	Medium to high heat	350° F.
Shallow-frying	Medium heat	350° F.
Deep-frying	High heat	425° F.
Red or white stewing	Low heat	225-250° F.
Steaming	Low heat	225-250° F.

Time will always be as the recipe directs. Timing in electric wok cookery is basically the same as top of the stove cooking. Check for doneness as you go. Use the recipe instructions for look, color and texture of the finished product as your ultimate guide.

The recipes in this book are written for the electric wok but they can be made with equal success in the top of stove wok. When the recipe says "set at ---° F." check the Conversion Chart and see what stove top setting is equal to that temperature. You are ready to cook in the electric wok when the light goes out. You are ready to cook on the top of the stove when the oil is hot and ripples when the wok is tilted or when the water is boiling or steam is rising.

With a little practice you will have no trouble converting these recipes or any of your own favorites for use on top of the stove.

About the recipes:

Flavoring oil: In many of the stir-fry recipes a clove or two of garlic is mashed. This means that you leave the clove whole and hit it with the side of a large knife or cleaver to release the aroma. This is often added to the hot oil with a slice of ginger, stir-fried, removed and discarded. You do this to give a hint of flavor to the oil. If you prefer a stronger flavor, mince both and do not discard after frying. Ginger is very strong and tends to dominate. Be prudent with its use.

Substitutions: If you do not have a particular ingredient or if you do not care for an ingredient in a recipe don't be afraid to substitute something similar or more to your liking.

Spices: The amounts of spices given in the recipes are generally on the conservative side. Try the recipe once before increasing the amounts. Some spices are very strong and you can always adjust the seasonings during cooking or make changes the next time around.

Dried ingredients: Dried mushrooms, cloud ear fungus and lilybuds must all be soaked for from 20 to 40 minutes. Be sure to leave time for this process. If these are not available use fresh mushrooms and even fresh wild tiger lily petals in summer. Of course you can simply substitute different vegetables in their place.

Mono-sodium glutamate: MSG is not used in any of the recipes because the author has found that it is not necessary and many people experience allergic reactions to it.

Preparation and cooking times and cooking technique: Preparation time and cooking time in each recipe are approximations given to be used as guides to help you determine which recipes will best fit into your schedule. They also will help you budget the time needed for preparation. Cooking technique is given to help plan the menu. It is a good idea to select items from different categories for variety and ease of preparation. Steamed, stewed and deep-fried items can be prepared ahead of time and reheated. Stir-fries require last minute preparation.

Push up sides of wok: This means the stir-fried ingredient is swept up the sides of the wok with a spatula or long handled spoon so that it remains in the wok but is no longer cooking. If the wok becomes too crowded you can remove and reserve these items. If you do this when the recipe does not instruct you to do so, reheat for one minute longer than the recipe indicates.

Doubling a recipe: This is generally not recommended since some recipes have many ingredients and twice the quantity would overload the wok. The vegetables would not be as crisp as they should be. Most recipes take only a few minutes so you can do it twice without that much of a problem. As an alternative, consider doing a different recipe to add more variety to the menu.

Recipes
From the East

The preparation of food is an art form in China. From the beginning of the country's recorded history it has been an integral part of the philosophy that shaped the lives of the people. Confucius elevated eating from a necessity to an art by making it a subject for discussion at distinguished gatherings. The ancient scholars, philosophers and writers were the composers of recipes and encyclopedias of culinary arts. According to legend, the Chinese Emperor Fu Hsi taught his people how to hunt and fish, cultivate the land and cook the food. From this time — twenty centuries before Christ — the wonders of the treasury of oriental cooking have been evolving.

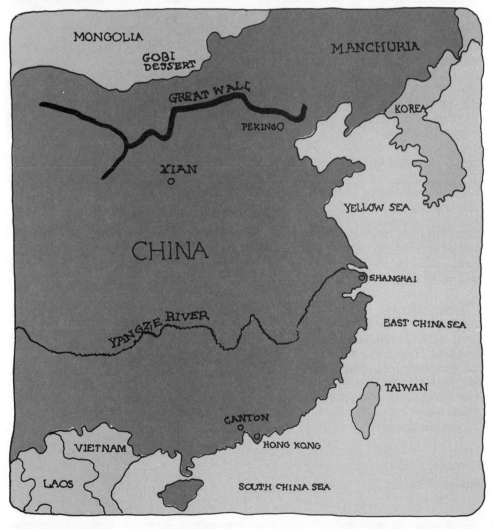

Oriental Sauces

Basic Oriental Sauce

Preparation time: 3 minutes
Cooking time: 2 to 4 minutes
Cooking technique: Simmering

2½ cups broth
½ cup soy sauce
¼ cup dry white wine or
  dry sherry

3 tablespoons cornstarch
2 teaspoons brown sugar

Combine all ingredients, pour mixture into wok when all stir-frying is completed. Simmer, stirring constantly until mixture thickens, about 1 minute. Return all reserved stir-fried ingredients to wok. Stir well to combine. Heat until hot, about 1 to 3 minutes.

Makes: 3¼ cups

Basic Honey Sauce

Preparation time: 3 minutes
Cooking time: 1 minute
Cooking technique: Simmering

¼ cup soy sauce
¼ cup white wine

¼ cup honey
¼ teaspoon garlic sauce

Combine all ingredients. Pour mixture into wok when all stir-frying is completed. Return all stir-fried ingredients to wok. Stir well to combine. Heat until hot, about 1 minute.

Makes: ¾ cups

Plum Sauce

Preparation time: 5 minutes
Cooking time: 5 minutes
Cooking technique: Simmering

1 jar (10 ounces) plum preserves
1 cup sweet and sour sauce
½ cup orange juice

1 teaspoon soy sauce
½ teaspoon hoisin sauce

Place all ingredients in wok. Set heat control at 250° F. Cover and simmer 5 minutes. Remove and cool. Store in clean jar for use as needed.

Makes: 3 cups

Basic Sweet and Sour Sauce

Preparation time: 3 minutes
Cooking time: 1 hour
Cooking technique: Simmering

2 tablespoons soy sauce	1 tablespoon brown sugar
¼ teaspoon powdered ginger	1 cup pineapple or orange juice
¼ cup white vinegar	

Combine all ingredients. Pour mixture into wok when all stir-frying is completed. Simmer, stirring constantly until mixture thickens, about 1 minute. Return all reserved stir-fried ingredients to wok. Stir well to combine. Heat until hot, about 1 minute.

Makes: 1¼ cups

Sweet and Sour Sauce

Preparation time: 10 minutes
Cooking time: 1 hour
Cooking technique: Simmering

1 jar (10 ounces) plum preserves	¾ cup light brown sugar
1 cup dried apricots, chopped	1 tablespoon chopped pimiento
1 can (1 pound) pear slices, with liquid	½ teaspoon powdered ginger
1 can (1 pound) peach slices, with liquid	⅓ cup honey
1 cup white vinegar	1 teaspoon salt
	1 clove garlic, minced

Place all ingredients into wok. Stir well to combine. Set heat control dial at 250° F. Simmer uncovered for 1 hour, stirring occasionally. Cool. Pour sauce into clean dry jar for use as needed. Refrigerate.

Makes: 1½ quarts

Mustard Sauce

Preparation time: 5 minutes

6 tablespoons Chinese prepared mustard	1 teaspoon vinegar
2 tablespoons mayonnaise	½ teaspoon sesame seeds
2 teaspoon sugar	½ teaspoon hoisin sauce
	2 scallions, minced

In a small bowl combine all ingredients. Serve as a dipping sauce for Peppery Meatballs, Fried Wonton or Egg Rolls.

Makes: About ½ cup

Northern China — Peking

Peking, the capital city of China, is in the North and is the center of government and the fountainhead of Chinese civilization. It is also an amalgam of Chinese peoples because of migration to this great cultural and intellectual center from all over China. This gathering of peoples has created an eclectic cuisine known as Mandarin.

There are two types of food in Peking, the food of the upper classes and that of the common man. The elite, including members of government, enjoy such gastronomic treats as Peking duck. In general, their food is well prepared in a gentle manner, using a good deal of wine which is blended with mild seasonings. In contrast, the everyday fare of the less affluent is simple and pungent, a hardy type of cooking which incorporates the use of scallions, onions, garlic, brown bean paste, soy sauce and vinegar. Noodles and pancakes are staples. Interestingly, rice is a luxury, a food eaten on a daily basis only by the well-to-do. It is only used on special occasions by the ordinary Chinese.

Of all the sections of China, the North has the least regional cuisine, probably because so many people have migrated there from other regions. Some say the northerners have taken many recipes from other areas of China and merely adjusted them to their tastes. This is not to say that there are not many classic Northern Chinese dishes. Some of the most famous Chinese recipes originated in the Henan and Shantung provinces.

The recipes in this chapter reflect the diversity of the peoples of the region and its topography.

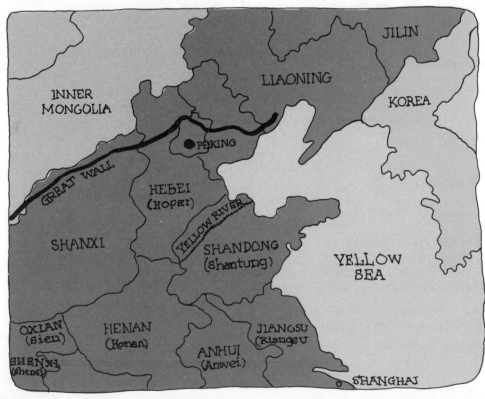

Chinese Meatballs with Spinach

Preparation time: 20 minutes
Cooking time: 20 minutes
Cooking technique: Shallow-frying, steaming

MEATBALL MIXTURE:

¾ pound ground pork
¾ pound ground beef
2 mushrooms, finely chopped
2 tablespoons bean sprouts, finely chopped
1 clove garlic, minced
2 scallions, minced

Vegetable oil

¼ cup finely chopped Chinese cabbage
1 tablespoon cornstarch
¼ teaspoon pepper
2 tablespoons soy sauce
1 teaspoon sesame oil
1 egg

SAUCE MIXTURE

1 cup beef broth
¼ cup soy sauce
1 tablespoon cornstarch

2 tablespoons white wine
½ teaspoon brown sugar
½ pound spinach, stems removed

In a large bowl, combine meatball mixture. Pour oil into wok. Set heat control dial at 350° F. While oil is heating, form meatball mixture into 40 (1-inch) meatballs. When light goes out add half of the meatballs and shallow-fry until meatballs are well browned on all sides. Remove meatballs to tempura rack or drain on absorbent paper towels. Fry remaining meatballs. Remove and reserve. Discard cooking oil. Wipe wok clean. Combine sauce mixture and pour into wok. Simmer, stirring constantly until sauce thickens, about 1 minute. Return meatballs to wok and stir well. Add spinach. Cover. Steam 2 minutes or until spinach is wilted.

Makes: 40 (1-inch) meatballs

Twice-cooked Pork Roast

Preparation time: 5 minutes
Cooking time: 2 hours
Cooking technique: Stewing, Deep-frying

1 boneless pork roast (2 pounds)
4 cups chicken broth
½ teaspoon Chinese five spice
  powder
¼ teaspoon pepper
¼ teaspoon powdered ginger

3 cloves garlic, minced
4 cups vegetable oil
1 egg, well beaten
¼ teaspoon garlic salt
3 tablespoons cornstarch

Place pork, broth, five spice powder, pepper, ginger and garlic in wok. Cover. Set heat control dial at 250 ° F. Simmer for 1½ hours. Remove pork and dry thoroughly. Discard broth. Wipe wok clean with a paper towel. Pour oil into wok. Set heat control dial at 425° F. While oil is heating combine egg and garlic salt. Roll roast in egg mixture and then in cornstarch to coat all sides. When light goes out deep-fry until golden brown, about 6 minutes per side. Serve with Sweet and Sour Sauce on page 23.

Makes: 4 to 6 servings

Paper-wrapped Chicken

Preparation time: 10 minutes
Marinating time: 2 hours
Cooking time: 25 minutes
Cooking technique: Deep-frying

MARINADE:
2 tablespoons soy sauce
2 tablespoons dry white wine or
  dry sherry
½ cup water

1 teaspoon brown sugar
⅛ teaspoon powdered ginger
Pinch Chinese five spice powder

1½ pounds boneless chicken
  breasts cut in 2-inch x ½-inch strips
4 cups vegetable oil
24 pieces (5 x 3½-inches each)
  unwaxed butcher paper, parchment
  or typing paper

12 scallions, white part only,
  cut in half lengthwise
6 water chestnuts, cut in 4 slices each
24 small snow pea pods

In a small bowl combine marinade ingredients. Marinate chicken for 2 hours. Remove chicken from marinade. Dry with paper towels. Pour oil into wok. Set heat control dial at 425° F. On each piece of paper place one each of the following: chicken strip, scallion half, water chestnut slice and snow pea pod. Roll up jelly roll style and twist edges as shown in illustration below. When light goes out fry 6 or 8 packets at a time, turning once, about 3 to 5 minutes. Drain on tempura rack or absorbent paper towels. Repeat with remaining packets. Serve packets and let diners unwrap their own. Serve with Plum Sauce, page 22.

Makes: 24

Recipes - Northern China

Brown Noodle Pancake with Chicken and Snow Peas

Preparation time: 10 minutes
Marinating time: 30 minutes
Cooking time: 15 minutes
Cooking technique: Stir-frying

MARINADE:

1 cup chicken broth
1 tablespoon cornstarch

1 tablespoon soy sauce
1 teaspoon brown sugar

2 chicken breasts, skinned, boned
   and cut in shreds
¾ cup vegetable oil
1 clove garlic, minced
3 scallions, sliced

¼ pound snow peas
1 can (8 ounces) water chestnuts,
   drained and sliced
¼ pound mushrooms, sliced
3 cups cooked brown Chinese
   noodles

In a large bowl combine marinade ingredients. Marinate chicken for 30 minutes. Pour ¼ cup oil into wok. Set heat control dial at 350° F. Add garlic and scallions and stir-fry 1 minute. Push up sides of wok. Add snow peas and water chestnuts and stir-fry 2 minutes. Push up sides of wok. Add mushrooms and stir-fry 1 minute. Push up sides of wok. Remove chicken from marinade. Reserve marinade. Add chicken to wok and stir-fry 2 minutes. Remove and reserve all stir-fried ingredients. Add remaining oil. When light goes out add noodles and press down to form pancake. Fry 3 minutes on first side, turn over and fry 2 minutes on second side. Remove pancake to a serving platter. Pour marinade into wok. Simmer, stirring constantly until mixture thickens, about 1 minute. Return vegetables and chicken to wok. Stir well to combine. Heat until hot, about 1 minute. Cut noodle pancake into 6 pieces. Pour vegetables and chicken over pancake.

Makes: 6 servings

Moo Shu Pork

Preparation time: 15 minutes
Cooking time: 10 minutes
Cooking technique: Stir-frying

¼ cup vegetable oil
¼ pound pork, shredded
1 clove garlic minced
1 small onion, chopped
1 tablespoon soy sauce
1 cup bok choy, chopped
10 dried tiger lily buds, presoaked
　and drained

4 cloud ear mushrooms
　presoaked and drained
3 eggs, lightly beaten
¼ cup chicken broth
1 teaspoon salt
¼ teaspoon pepper
½ teaspoon sugar
Chinese Pancakes

Pour 2 tablespoons oil into wok. Set heat control dial at 350° F. When light goes out add pork and stir-fry 3 minutes. Push up sides of wok. Add garlic, onion and soy sauce and stir-fry 30 seconds. Push up sides of wok. Add remaining oil. When light goes out add bok choy, lilies and cloud ears and stir-fry 1 minute. Remove all ingredients and reserve. Add eggs and scramble. Before eggs set add broth, salt, pepper, sugar and reserved ingredients. Stir until combined. Serve with Chinese Pancakes.

Makes: Filling for 8 (6-inch) pancakes.

Chinese Pancakes

Preparation time: 15 minutes
Cooking time: 20 minutes
Cooking technique: Pan-frying

1 cup boiling water
2 cups all-purpose flour
Vegetable oil

In a large bowl pour boiling water into flour. Stir well to combine. On a lightly floured board knead the dough until smooth and elastic, about 5 minutes. Form into a 16-inch log. Cut log into 16 one-inch pieces. Roll 8 pieces of dough into 6-inch pancakes. Lightly oil the top of these pancakes leaving a ½-inch outer rim unoiled. Roll the remaining 8 pancakes. Place an unoiled pancake on top of an oiled one and roll with a rolling pin to seal. You will have 8 finished pancakes. Set heat control dial to 325° F. Wipe bottom of wok lightly with vegetable oil. When light goes out cook pancakes one at a time until lightly browned, about 2 minutes per side. Make a pocket in one side of each pancake and fill with *Moo Shu* Pork. Serve immediately.

Makes: 8 servings

Meatball Soup with Chinese Noodles

Preparation time: 10 minutes
Cooking time: 40 minutes
Cooking techniques: Shallow-frying, Simmering

½ pound ground pork
½ pound ground beef
2 ounces bean curd
1 egg
1 clove garlic, minced
2 scallions, minced
4 mushrooms, minced
1 teaspoon salt

¼ teaspoon pepper
⅓ cup vegetable oil
¼ pound Chinese cabbage, cut
   in 1-inch pieces
1 can (8 ounces) water chestnuts,
   drained and sliced
6 cups beef broth
1½ cups Chinese noodles

In a large bowl combine pork, beef, bean curd, egg, garlic, scallions, mushrooms, salt and pepper. Form mixture into 54 1-inch meatballs. Pour oil into wok. Set heat control dial at 350° F. When light goes out shallow-fry meatballs until well browned, about 5 minutes. Remove meatballs and all but 2 tablespoons of oil from wok. Add cabbage and water chestnuts and stir-fry 1 minute. Return meatballs to wok. Add broth. Cover. Turn heat control dial to 250° F. Simmer for 20 minutes. Add noodles. Cover. Simmer 10 minutes.

Makes: 8 servings

Lamb-filled Dumplings

Preparation time: 30 minutes
Cooking time: 20 minutes
Cooking technique: Shallow-frying

2 cups all-purpose flour
⅔ cup boiling water
¼ cup cold water

FILLING:
½ pound ground lamb
1 leek, chopped
½ cup chopped Chinese cabbage
½ cup vegetable oil

2 tablespoons soy sauce
1 teaspoon sesame oil
1 clove garlic, minced

In a large bowl combine flour and hot and cold water. With lightly floured hands knead well to form a soft ball. Cover. Allow to stand for 15 minutes. While dough is standing prepare filling by combining all ingredients. Roll out dough as thin as possible on a lightly floured board. Cut into 24 (3-inch) circles with a biscuit cutter or the top of a glass. Pour oil into wok. Set heat control dial at 350 ° F. While oil is heating spoon about 1 heaping teaspoon of filling in the center of each dough round. Fold over and crimp edges with a fork to seal. When light goes out add half of the dumplings to wok and shallow-fry until well browned, about 3 to 5 minutes per side. Drain on tempura rack or absorbent paper towels. Add remaining dumplings and shallow-fry as before. Serve with vegetables as a main course.

Makes: 24 dumplings

Recipes - Northern China.

Stir-fry Marinated Lamb

Preparation time: 10 minutes
Marinating time: 1 hour
Cooking time: 5 minutes
Cooking technique: Stir-frying

MARINADE:

2 tablespoons soy sauce
1½ cups chicken broth
1 teaspoon brown sugar

1 tablespoon cornstarch
1 tablespoon dry white wine or
  dry sherry

1 pound boneless lamb, thinly sliced
1 tablespoon vegetable oil

3 cloves garlic, minced
3 scallions, minced

Combine marinade ingredients. Marinate lamb for 1 hour. Reserve marinade. Pour oil into wok. Set heat control dial at 350° F. When light goes out add garlic, scallions and lamb and stir-fry 3 minutes. Add marinade to wok. Simmer, stirring constantly until mixture thickens, about 1 minute. Serve immediately.

Makes: 3 to 4 servings

Peking-style Egg *Fu Yung*

Preparation time: 5 minutes
Cooking time: 3 minutes
Cooking technique: Stir-frying

2 tablespoons vegetable oil
6 water chestnuts, diced
½ cup sliced bamboo shoots, diced
2 scallions, minced
2 tablespoons chicken broth

1 teaspoon dry white wine or
  dry sherry
½ teaspoon salt
dash pepper
4 egg yolks

Pour oil into wok. Set heat control dial at 300° F. Combine remaining ingredients. When light goes out pour mixture into wok. Stir-fry until eggs are firmly set. Serve immediately.

Makes: 2 to 3 servings

Fish Filets with Peking Lobster Sauce

Preparation time: 5 minutes
Cooking time: 10 minutes
Cooking techniques: Steaming, Simmering

2 cups water
1 pound flounder filets
½ teaspoon salt
⅛ teaspoon pepper
2 tablespoons butter or margarine
2 tablespoons all-purpose flour
1 cup chicken broth

1 tablespoon lemon juice
1 tablespoon dry white wine
1 can lobster meat (6 ounces), drained
½ teaspoon salt
⅛ teaspoon pepper
½ cup heavy cream

Place steamer insert or rack into wok. Pour water into wok. Place fish on rack and sprinkle with salt and pepper. Set heat control dial at 250° F. Steam for 5 minutes. Remove fish to platter and cover with aluminum foil. Remove insert and discard water. Wipe wok dry. Place butter into wok. Set heat control dial at 250° F. When butter melts (do not wait for light to go out), stir in flour to form a paste. Add broth, lemon juice, wine, lobster, salt and pepper. Stir well to combine. Heat until hot. Add cream, stir, simmer for 20 seconds. Turn heat control dial to "off." Pour sauce over fish. Serve immediately.

Makes: 4 servings

Peking Precious Pot

Preparation time: 20 minutes
Cooking time: 10 minutes to 1 hour
Cooking technique: Simmering

8 cups beef broth
1 pound flank steak, angle-cut into
   thin slices
2 chicken breasts, skinned, boned
   and cut in 1-inch pieces
¾ pound shrimp, shelled, cleaned
   and deveined

1 pound fish steaks, cut in
   1-inch chunks
1 pound Chinese cabbage
½ pound spinach
12 scallions, whole white part only
½ pound bok choy, cut in 1-inch
   pieces
½ pound cellophane noodles

Pour broth into wok. Set heat control dial at 250° F. While broth is heating prepare ingredients, dividing them into 6 individual servings. Supply each guest with a tray of ingredients, chop sticks or a long handled fondue fork and small bowls of Mustard Sauce (pp 23), Plum Sauce (pp 22) and Sweet and Sour Sauce (pp 23), for dipping. When broth is boiling cooking can begin. Each guest dips his own food into the broth, cooking to desired doneness. When all food is cooked place cellophane noodles into broth and cook until soft, about 10 minutes. Serve each guest a cup of soup.

Makes: 6 servings

Southern China — Canton

Canton, a seaport in southern China, was the gateway to the West when the European nations began to trade with China in the 16th century. It has been a center for foreign trade since ancient times. The vast majority of the first Chinese immigrants to Europe and America were from the southern provinces. Which is probably why we in the United States usually think of Chinese food as it is prepared in the Cantonese style.

When gold was discovered in California in 1849 the news travelled quickly to China. Many Chinese emigrated to California to seek their fortune in a land known to them as "the land of the Golden Mountains." They came as laborers to build the railroads and to dig for gold. They also worked as houseboys and cooks, thereby introducing their cuisine and adapting it to their new land.

The coastline of the southern region is irregular and in some areas the land is quite mountainous. In some sections people live on boats and depend on the sea for most of their food. By contrast, other parts of the South depend entirely on the land. The climate is tropical. Temperatures are rarely below 40° F. and snow is found only in the mountains. The summers are hot and humid. As many as three agricultural harvests a year are possible in these areas.

Stir-frying was perfected by the Cantonese. They are masters of blending the flavors of meat and vegetables in delicately flavored sauces enriched by soy sauce, a hint of ginger and dash of sugar. The cuisine of the South is not all mild. Strong sauces laced with garlic, fermented black beans, curry and oyster sauce are also found. Finally the sweet and sour dishes make use of the tropical fruits grown there, including pineapple and lichee.

This chapter's recipes highlight the Cantonese style of cooking. If, like millions of other Americans, you have eaten in Chinese restaurants, you will find this section most familiar. Also included, however, are dishes from other southern provinces. They will be less familiar but equally delicious.

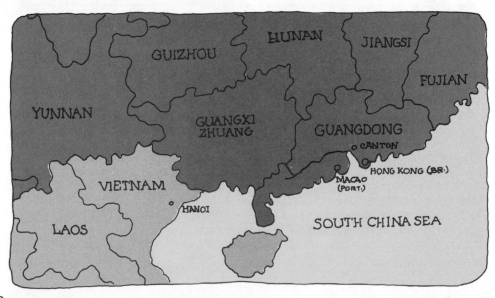

Chicken with Snow Peas and Peanuts

Preparation time: 20 minutes
Cooking time: 15 minutes
Cooking technique: Stir-frying

½ cup vegetable oil
½ cup shelled peanuts
1 clove garlic, mashed
1 slice ginger root, cut ¼-inch thick
2 whole chicken breasts, skinned and
   boned, cut in ½-inch pieces
½ pound snow peas

¼ pound mushrooms, sliced
3 tablespoons cornstarch
2½ cups chicken broth or stock
¼ cup soy sauce
2 tablespoons dry white wine or
   dry sherry
¼ teaspoon pepper

Pour 2 tablespoons oil into wok. Set heat control dial at 350° F. When light goes out add peanuts and stir-fry 1 minute. Remove and reserve. Add garlic and ginger root and stir-fry 1 minute. Remove and discard. Add chicken to wok and stir-fry 3 minutes, push cooked pieces up the sides of the wok as they cook. Remove and reserve. Add more oil if needed. When light goes out, add snow pea pods and stir-fry for 1 minute. Remove and reserve. Stir-fry mushrooms for 30 seconds. Remove. Combine remaining ingredients and pour mixture into wok. Simmer, stirring constantly until mixture thickens, about 1 minute. Return all ingredients to wok. Stir well to combine. Heat until hot, about 1 minute. Serve immediately over rice.

Makes: 4 servings

Beef with Snow Peas, Tomatoes and Onions

Preparation time: 15 minutes
Marinating time: 30 minutes
Cooking time: 10 minutes
Cooking technique: Stir-frying

MARINADE:

¼ cup soy sauce
¼ cup water
1 cup chicken broth
1 tablespoon cornstarch
2 tablespoons dry white wine

1 clove garlic, mashed
1 teaspoon brown sugar
¼ teaspoon fermented black bean, minced

1 pound flank steak, angle-cut into thin slices
¼ cup vegetable oil

2 medium onions cut into ¼-inch wedges
¼ pound snow peas
2 medium tomatoes, cut in ½-inch wedges

In a large bowl combine marinade ingredients. Marinate beef slices in marinade for 30 minutes at room temperature or three hours in the refrigerator. While meat is marinating prepare remaining ingredients. Pour 2 tablespoons oil into wok. Set heat control dial at 350° F. When light goes out add onions. Stir-fry 3 minutes. Push up sides of wok. Add snow peas, stir-fry 1 minute. Remove onions and peas and reserve. Add more oil if needed. When light goes out add meat five or six slices at a time. Stir-fry 1 minute. Push up sides of wok. Reserve marinade to be used as cooking sauce. Add oil as needed and continue to stir-fry until all meat is cooked. Remove and reserve. Pour reserved marinade into wok. Simmer, stirring constantly until mixture thickens, about 1 minute. Return meat and vegetables to wok along with tomatoes, stir well to combine. Heat until hot, about 1 minute. Serve immediately over rice with crispy Chinese noodles.

Makes: 4 servings

Deep-fried Spareribs

Preparation time: 10 minutes
Marinating time: 1 hour
Cooking time: ½ hour
Cooking technique: Deep-frying

MARINADE:

1 can beef broth (10 ounces)
¼ cup orange juice
¼ cup soy sauce
½ cup water
1 tablespoon cornstarch
1 tablespoon brown sugar
1 tablespoon fermented black beans

2 tablespoons dry white wine or
  dry sherry
1 slice ginger root, cut ¼-inch thick
1 clove garlic, minced
2 scallions, chopped
1 rack (1½ to 2 pounds) pork spareribs cut into pieces

3 cups vegetable oil
¾ cup cornstarch

SAUCE:

¼ cup orange juice
¼ cup Plum Sauce

¼ cup duck sauce
1 teaspoon hoisin sauce

In a large bowl combine marinade ingredients. Marinate ribs for 1 hour at room temperature or 6 hours in refrigerator. Remove ribs and dredge them in cornstarch shaking off any excess. Pour in oil. Set heat control dial at 425° F. When light goes out carefully place 6 to 8 spareribs in wok. Fry 8 minutes or until they are deep golden brown. Drain on tempura rack or absorbent paper towels. When oil is hot add remaining ribs. Fry until well browned. While ribs are frying combine sauce ingredients. After ribs have drained brush them with sauce. Serve remaining sauce.

Makes: 4 servings

Beef with Carrots, Celery and Chinese Cabbage

Preparation time: 40 minutes
Cooking time: 20 minutes
Cooking technique: Stir-frying

⅓ cup vegetable oil
2 cloves garlic, mashed
1 slice ginger root, ¼-inch thick
3 carrots, angle-cut into thin slices
5 stalks celery, angle-cut into
   thin slices
2 cups chopped Chinese
   cabbage
8 scallions, angle-cut into
   thin slices

1 pound flank steak, angle-cut
   into thin slices
2½ cups beef broth
½ cup soy sauce
¼ cup dry white wine or dry sherry
3 tablespoons cornstarch
2 teaspoons brown sugar

Pour 2 tablespoons oil into wok. Set heat control at 350° F. When light goes out add garlic and ginger root, stir-fry 1 minute. Remove and discard. Add carrots and celery and stir-fry 3 minutes. Remove and reserve. Add more oil if needed. When light goes out add Chinese cabbage and scallions. Stir-fry 1 minute. Remove and reserve. Add flank steak to wok, stir-fry 3 minutes. Remove and reserve. Combine remaining ingredients and pour mixture into wok. Simmer, stirring constantly until mixture thickens, about 1 minute. Return all ingredients to wok. Stir well to combine. Heat until hot, about 1 minute. Serve immediately over cooked rice, if desired.

Makes: 6 servings

Stir-fry Vegetables

Preparation time: 15 minutes
Cooking time: 5 minutes
Cooking technique: Stir-frying

½ cup vegetable oil
1 clove garlic, mashed
1 slice ginger root, cut
   ¼-inch thick
2 carrots, angle-cut,
   ¼-inch thick
2 celery stalks, angle-cut,
   ¼-inch thick
1 onion, thinly sliced

1 can (8 ounces) water chestnuts,
   sliced and drained
1 medium zucchini, angle-cut,
   ¼-inch thick
¼ pound mushrooms, sliced
1 medium tomato, cut in wedges
1 teaspoon salt
⅛ teaspoon pepper

Pour 2 tablespoons oil into wok. Set heat control dial at 350° F. Add garlic and ginger root and stir-fry 1 minute. Remove and discard. Add carrots and celery and stir-fry 3 minutes. Push up sides of wok. Add onions and stir-fry 1 minute. Push up sides of wok. Add more oil if needed. When light goes out add water chestnuts and zucchini, stir-frying 1½ minutes. Push up sides of wok. Add mushrooms and tomatoes and stir-fry 30 seconds. Stir in vegetables from sides of wok to combine. Serve with salt and pepper, immediately.

Makes: 6 servings

Chicken with Dried Black Mushrooms and Tiger Lily Buds

Preparation time: 30 minutes
Cooking time: 10 minutes
Cooking technique: Steaming

1 clove garlic, mashed
1 slice ginger root,
   ¼-inch thick
2 scallions
1 cup chicken broth
2 tablespoons dry white wine
   or dry sherry
½ teaspoon sugar
⅛ teaspoon pepper

2 tablespoons soy sauce
3 whole chicken breasts, skinned,
   boned and cut in 3-inch pieces
8 dried black mushrooms,
   soaked for 20 minutes
12 dried tiger lily buds,
   soaked for 20 minutes
1 tablespoon cornstarch
¼ cup water

Place garlic, ginger root, scallions, broth, wine, sugar, pepper and soy sauce in wok. Place steamer insert or rack in wok, put chicken on rack. Place pre-soaked mushrooms and tiger lily buds on top of chicken. Cover. Set heat control dial at 250° F. Steam for 10 minutes or until juices of chicken run clear. Remove chicken and vegetables to serving platter. Combine cornstarch and water. Pour mixture into wok. Simmer, stirring constantly until mixture thickens, about 20 seconds. Pour over chicken. Serve immediately.

Makes: 6 servings

Ground Beef with Snow Peas and Water Chestnuts

Preparation time: 20 minutes
Cooking time: 10 minutes
Cooking technique: Stir-frying

1 pound ground beef
1 tablespoon soy sauce
1 tablespoon dry white wine
   or dry sherry
1 tablespoon cornstarch
1 tablespoon water
1 clove garlic, mashed
1 slice ginger root, ¼-inch thick

½ pound snow peas
1 can (8 ounces) water chestnuts,
   drained and sliced
3 scallions sliced
1 cup beef broth
1 tablespoon oyster sauce
1 tablespoon cornstarch

In a large bowl combine beef, soy sauce, wine, cornstarch and water. Set heat control dial at 350° F. When light goes out add ground beef. Stir-fry for 3 minutes or until well browned. Remove and reserve. Add garlic and ginger root and stir-fry 1 minute. Remove and discard. Add snow peas and stir-fry 1 minute. Remove and reserve. Add water chestnuts and scallions and stir-fry 1 minute. Remove and reserve. Combine remaining ingredients and pour mixture into wok. Simmer, stirring constantly until mixture thickens, about 1 minute. Return all ingredients to wok. Stir well to combine. Heat until hot, about 1 minute. Serve immediately with rice or Chinese noodles.

Makes: 4 servings

Egg Rolls

Preparation time: 20 minutes
Cooking time: 8 minutes
Cooking technique: Stir-frying, Deep-frying

2 tablespoons vegetable oil
¼ pound boneless pork, diced
1 small onion, minced
1 clove garlic, minced
½ cup bean sprouts, chopped
⅓ cup spinach

2 mushrooms, minced
1 stalk celery, minced
2 teaspoons soy sauce
4 large egg roll wrappers
½ teaspoon cornstarch
3 cups vegetable oil

Pour 2 tablespoons oil into wok. Set heat control dial at 350° F. When light goes out add pork and stir-fry 2 minutes. Add onions and garlic and continue to stir-fry 1 minute. Remove and allow to cool for 5 minutes. When mixture is cool add bean sprouts, spinach, mushrooms, celery and soy sauce. Mix well to combine. Wipe wok clean with a paper towel. Pour oil into wok. Set heat control dial at 425° F. While oil is heating dust bottom side of egg roll wrappers with cornstarch. With one corner of wrapper square facing you, place ¼ cup of filling slightly below the center of the square. Take the corner closest to you and fold up towards the center of the square over the filling. Tuck the point under the filling and roll one half turn (180°). Fold side corners in toward the center. Continue to roll to form a cylinder. Moisten last corner with water to seal. See illustration on next page. Repeat until all egg rolls are filled. When light goes out fry egg rolls until golden brown, about 3 to 5 minutes, turning once. Drain on tempura rack or absorbent paper towels.

Makes: 4 large egg rolls

Note: If available wrappers are smaller, use less filling and prepare as many as filling will allow. Fry until golden brown.

How to roll and seal egg rolls

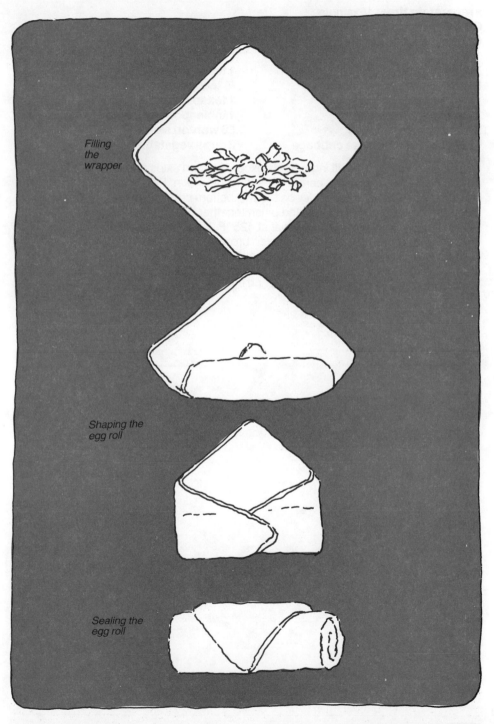

Filling the wrapper

Shaping the egg roll

Sealing the egg roll

Fried *Wontons*

Preparation time: 15 minutes
Cooking time: 45 minutes
Cooking technique: Deep-frying

½ pound ground pork
6 water chestnuts, minced
1 clove garlic, minced
3 scallions, minced
3 mushrooms, minced
¾ cup minced Chinese cabbage

1 teaspoon salt
½ teaspoon brown sugar
1 teaspoon sesame oil
1 tablespoon soy sauce
36 wonton skins
3 cups vegetable oil

In a large bowl combine all ingredients except wonton skins and oil. Place about 1 tablespoon of mixture in the center of each wonton skin. Fold in half diagonally with corners even. Brush a little water on the two bottom corners and fold bottom corners toward each other. Overlap tips and pinch together. See illustration on next page. Pour oil into wok. Set heat control dial at 425° F. When light goes out place 5 or 6 wontons into oil and deep-fry until golden brown, about 3 to 5 minutes. Drain on tempura rack or absorbent paper towels. Continue to fry until all are cooked. Serve immediately with Plum Sauce (page 22), Mustard Sauce (page 23), and Sweet and Sour Sauce (page 23).

Makes: 36

How to roll and seal *wontons*

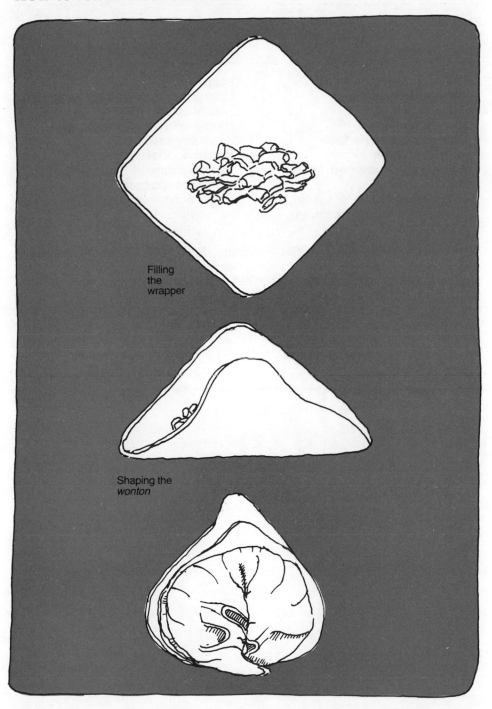

Filling
the
wrapper

Shaping the
wonton

Sub Gum

Preparation time: 30 minutes
Cooking time: 20 minutes
Cooking technique: Stir-frying

2 tablespoons vegetable oil
1 clove garlic, crushed
1 slice ginger root,
  sliced ¼-inch thick
¼ pound boneless pork,
  cut in thin strips
1 chicken breast, skinned, boned,
  and cut in strips
¼ pound cooked ham, cut in strips
1 can (8 ounces) water chestnuts,
  drained and sliced

1 cup bean sprouts
1 can (8½ ounces) sliced
  bamboo shoots
1½ cups chicken broth
¼ cup soy sauce
2 tablespoons dry white wine
  or dry sherry
3 tablespoons cornstarch
1 teaspoon brown sugar

Pour 2 tablespoons oil into wok. Set heat control dial at 350° F. When light goes out add garlic and ginger root. Stir-fry 1 minute. Remove and discard. Add pork and stir-fry 3 minutes. Add chicken and stir-fry 2 minutes. Push up sides of wok. Add ham and stir-fry 1 minute. Remove meats and reserve. Add oil if needed. When light goes out add water chestnuts, bean sprouts and bamboo shoots and stir-fry 1 minute. Remove and reserve. Combine remaining ingredients and pour mixture into wok. Simmer, stirring constantly until mixture thickens, about 1 minute. Return all ingredients to wok. Stir well to combine. Heat until hot, about 1 minute. Serve immediately with Chinese noodles.

Makes: 4 servings

Egg Drop Soup

Preparation time: 10 minutes
Cooking time: 25 minutes
Cooking technique: Simmering

1 tablespoon vegetable oil
¼ pound boneless pork,
  cut in thin shreds
3 scallions, chopped
8 cups chicken stock
¼ cup cornstarch
1 teaspoon brown sugar

½ teaspoon salt
1 tablespoon dry white wine
  or dry sherry
1 tablespoon soy sauce
3 eggs
¼ cup water

Pour oil into wok. Set heat control dial at 350° F. When light goes out add pork and stir-fry until browned, about 3 minutes. Add scallions and stir-fry 1 minute. Remove and reserve. Combine stock, cornstarch, sugar, salt, wine and soy sauce. Pour into wok. Turn heat control dial to 250° F. and simmer, uncovered, until soup comes to a boil and thickens, about 20 minutes. Beat eggs and water together and pour them in steady stream into the soup, stirring slowly so that eggs form thin threads. Simmer 5 minutes. Garnish with pork and scallions.

Makes: 9 cups

Fish with Onions, Mushrooms and Peas

Preparation time: 10 minutes
Cooking time: 10 minutes
Cooking technique: Stir-frying

¼ cup vegetable oil
1 pound flounder or sole filets,
  cut in 1-inch strips
2 tablespoons cornstarch
1 clove garlic, crushed
1 slice ginger root,
  cut ¼-inch thick
1 medium onion, cut in strips

1 can (8½ ounces) bamboo shoots,
  drained
¼ pound mushrooms, sliced
½ cup frozen peas, thawed
2 tablespoons soy sauce
2 tablespoons dry white wine
1 teaspoon sugar

Pour 2 tablespoons oil into wok. Set heat control dial at 350° F. Dredge fish pieces in cornstarch. When light goes out add garlic and ginger root and stir-fry 1 minute. Remove and discard. Add fish and stir-fry 2 to 3 minutes or until lightly browned. Remove and reserve. Add more oil if needed. When light goes out add onions and stir-fry 2 minutes. Push up sides of wok. Add bamboo shoots, mushrooms and peas and stir-fry 1 minute. Remove and reserve. Combine remaining ingredients. Pour mixture into wok. Simmer, stirring constantly until mixture thickens, about 1 minute. Return all ingredients to wok except fish. Stir to combine. Heat until hot, about 1 minute. Serve immediately over fish.

Makes: 4 servings

Cantonese Deep-fried Lemon Chicken

Preparation time: 20 minutes
Marinating time: 30 minutes
Cooking time: 15 minutes
Cooking Technique: Deep-frying

MARINADE:

¼ cup water
3 tablespoons soy sauce
2 tablespoons dry white wine
   or dry sherry

1 clove garlic, minced
1 slice ginger root, cut ¼-inch thick
1 teaspoon sesame oil

3 whole chicken breasts, skinned,
   boned and cut in 2-inch strips
3 cups vegetable oil

1 egg, well beaten
3 tablespoons cornstarch

SAUCE:

1¼ cup chicken broth
2 tablespoons lemon juice

1 tablespoon cornstarch
1 tablespoon sugar

In a large bowl combine all marinade ingredients. Place chicken in bowl and marinate for 30 minutes. Pour oil into wok. Set heat control dial at 425° F. While oil is heating remove chicken from marinade. Discard marinade. Dip chicken in egg and then into cornstarch. When light goes out add half of the chicken to wok and deep-fry until golden brown, about 3 minutes. When light goes out fry the remaining chicken. Drain on tempura rack or absorbent paper towels. Combine sauce ingredients. Carefully discard oil. Wipe wok clean with a paper towel. Pour sauce mixture into wok. Turn heat control to 350° F. Simmer, stirring constantly until sauce thickens, about 1 minute. Return chicken to wok. Stir well to combine. Heat until hot, about 3 to 5 minutes. Serve immediately.

Makes: 4 servings

Lobster Cantonese

Preparation time: 5 minutes
Cooking time: 15 minutes
Cooking technique: Steaming, Stir-frying

2 cups water
2 pounds lobster tails
2 tablespoons vegetable oil
¼ pound ground pork
1 clove garlic, minced
3 scallions, chopped
¼ teaspoon fermented black beans

2 tablespoons soy sauce
1 cup chicken broth
2 tablespoons cornstarch
2 tablespoons white wine
1 teaspoon vinegar
1 egg, well beaten

Place steamer insert or rack into wok. Pour water into wok. Put lobster tails on rack. Set heat control dial at 250° F. Cover. Steam for 5 to 8 minutes or until meat is tender. Remove tails and insert from wok. Discard water. Allow lobster tails to cool. Remove meat, cut into bite-size chunks and reserve. Pour oil into wok, add ground pork and stir-fry 1 minute. Push up sides of wok. Add garlic, scallions and black beans and stir-fry 1 minute. Push up sides of wok. Add lobster meat and stir-fry 30 seconds. Push up sides of wok. Combine remaining ingredients except egg and pour mixture into wok. Simmer, stirring constantly until mixture thickens, about 1 minute. Stir in all ingredients from sides of wok. Heat until hot, about 1 minute. Turn heat control dial to "off," stir in egg. Serve immediately.

Makes: 4 servings

Beef and Onions with Oyster Sauce

Preparation time: 10 minutes
Marinating time: 1 hour
Cooking time: 10 minutes
Cooking technique: Stir-frying

MARINADE:
1½ cups beef broth
¼ cup oyster sauce
2 tablespoons cornstarch

2 tablespoons soy sauce
2 tablespoons dry white wine

1 pound flank steak, angle-cut
  into thin slices
¼ cup vegetable oil

2 medium onions, cut in strips
3 cloves garlic, minced

In a large bowl combine marinade ingredients. Marinate meat for 1 hour. Remove meat from marinade; reserve marinade. Pour 2 tablespoons oil into wok. Set heat control dial at 350° F. When light goes out add onions and stir-fry until lightly browned, about 2 minutes. Add garlic and stir-fry 30 seconds. Push up sides of wok. Add meat and stir-fry 2 minutes. Push up sides of wok. Pour marinade into wok, simmer, stirring constantly until mixture thickens, about 1 minute. Stir in meat and onions. Heat until hot, about 1 minute. Serve immediately.

Makes: 4 servings

Sea Bass with Black Bean Sauce

Preparation time: 5 minutes
Cooking time: 25 minutes
Cooking technique: Steaming, Stir-frying

1 whole sea bass (1½ to 2 pounds)
2 cups water
2 tablespoons vegetable oil
1 clove garlic, mashed
1 slice ginger root, cut ¼-inch thick
3 scallions, sliced
2 tablespoons prepared black bean
   sauce

1 cup chicken broth
2 tablespoons white wine
1 teaspoon sugar
1 tablespoon soy sauce
2 teaspoons cornstarch
1 teaspoon sesame oil

Place steamer insert or rack into wok. Pour water into wok. Place fish on insert. Cover. Set heat control dial at 250° F. Steam until fish flakes easily with fork, about 15 to 18 minutes. Remove fish to platter and cover with aluminum foil. Remove insert and discard water. Wipe wok with a paper towel. Pour oil into wok. Set heat control dial at 350° F. When light goes out add garlic and ginger root and stir-fry 1 minute. Remove and discard. Add scallions and stir-fry 1 minute. Push up sides of wok. Combine remaining ingredients and pour mixture into wok. Stir in scallions. Simmer, stirring constantly until mixture thickens, about 1 minute. Pour over reserved fish.

Makes: 4 to 6 servings

Chicken *Lo Mein*

Preparation time: 20 minutes
Cooking time: 10 minutes
Cooking technique: Stir-frying

¼ pound Chinese noodles, cooked
¼ cup vegetable oil
1 clove garlic, minced
3 scallions, minced
½ pound bok choy,
   cut in ¼-inch slices
2 whole chicken breasts, skinned,
   boned and cut in thin strips

½ cup chicken broth
2 tablespoons soy sauce
1 tablespoon oyster sauce
1 teaspoon salt
1 teaspoon sugar
¼ teaspoon pepper

Cook Chinese noodles according to package directions and reserve. Pour 2 tablespoons oil into wok. Set heat control dial at 350° F. When light goes out add garlic and scallions and stir-fry 1 minute. Push up sides of wok. Add bok choy and stir-fry 2 minutes. Push up sides of wok. Add remaining oil if needed. When light goes out add chicken and stir-fry 3 minutes. Add remaining ingredients and noodles. Stir well to combine. Heat until hot, about 2 minutes. Serve immediately.

Makes: 6 servings

Cantonese-style Egg *Fu Yung*

Preparation time: 10 minutes
Cooking time: 10 minutes
Cooking technique: Stir-frying

⅓ cup vegetable oil
½ small chicken breast,
   cut into thin strips
3 scallions, sliced
3 mushrooms, thinly sliced

½ cup bamboo shoots
4 eggs
½ teaspoon salt
⅛ teaspoon pepper

Pour 2 tablespoons oil into wok. Set heat control dial at 350° F. When light goes out add chicken and stir-fry 2 minutes. Push up sides of wok and add scallions, mushrooms and bamboo shoots. Stir-fry 1 minute. Remove and reserve. Combine eggs, salt and pepper. Pour remaining oil into wok. Turn heat control to 300° F. When light goes out add egg mixture. Do not stir. When eggs are almost dry sprinkle reserved ingredients on top of eggs. Continue to cook without stirring until eggs are dry on top and browned on bottom. Fold eggs over to form omelet. Serve with soy sauce.

Makes: 3 to 4 servings

Apricot-filled Deep-fried Cakes

Preparation time: 10 minutes
Cooking time: 55 minutes
Cooking technique: Simmering, Crêpe-making, Deep-frying

FILLING:
8 ounces dried apricots, finely
   chopped
½ cup brown sugar
½ cup water

⅔ cup almonds, finely chopped
¼ tablespoon orange juice
1 teaspoon lemon extract

PANCAKES:
1 cup all-purpose flour
½ teaspoon salt

1 egg, well beaten
1 cup water

3 cups vegetable oil
confectioners' sugar

Pour filling ingredients into wok. Set heat control dial at 225° F. Allow mixture to simmer for 3 minutes, stirring occasionally. Remove filling from wok and allow to cool. Clean wok. While filling is cooling combine pancake batter. Set heat control dial at 325° F. Dip a paper towel into a small amount of vegetable oil and wipe bottom surface of wok. When light goes out pour 2 tablespoons of batter into wok. Tilt to coat ½ of the bottom of wok making pancakes as thin as possible. Allow pancake to set, but not brown, about 1 minute. Turn and bake on second side. Remove to a platter. Continue to cook until all pancakes are made. Place 1 tablespoon of filling on the center of each pancake. Fold over and crimp edges. While you are filling pancakes, pour oil into wok. Set heat control dial at 425° F. When light goes out add one half of the pancakes to wok and deep-fry until golden brown, about 5 minutes. Drain on tempura rack or absorbent paper towels. Continue until all cakes are fried. Cool. Dust with confectioners' sugar.

Makes: about 24

Eastern China — Shanghai

In the eastern region of China lowlands are dominated by water. There are many shallow lakes and much swamp land. This, coupled with a mild climate is perfect for growing rice. Much of China's rice is grown here and is therefore the staple of the diet.

The cooking of this region is varied because it is hard to travel. People are isolated from each other and each small community has its own traditions and dialect. You will find delicious delicate pastries fit for an emperor. (These were probably served to the Emperor and his court in the 13th century when the capital of China was moved from the North to Hangchow because of the Mongolian invasions.) There are also subtle stir-fried as well as more robust stewed dishes. These hardy recipes are the basis for the home-style everyday cooking that is most popular here.

Stewing and red-simmering, a type of cooking in which foods are steeped in liquid for a long period of time to blend the various flavors, are the major components of this style cuisine. There are many popular red cooked dishes, and to combat the saltiness of soy sauce used in them, many are prepared with large amounts of sugar.

In the sections of the region dominated by water a large amount of fish is eaten. In the Fujian area, for example, fish is cooked using a small amount of soy sauce, vinegar and scallions. Many students of Chinese cuisine rank the Fujian school of cooking as a classic style, one to be especially savored and enjoyed.

Because of the abundance of rice, the production of some of the finest rice wine is achieved in this region. A spicy sweet paste is made from the sediment of these wines. It is used to flavor meat, fish and poultry. This paste is generally available commercially or can be prepared in your wok using the recipe on page 53.

For a change of pace from the stir-fried dishes of Canton, or to complete a menu for an oriental dinner party, try several of the recipes in this chapter. They have a unique flavor you will enjoy.

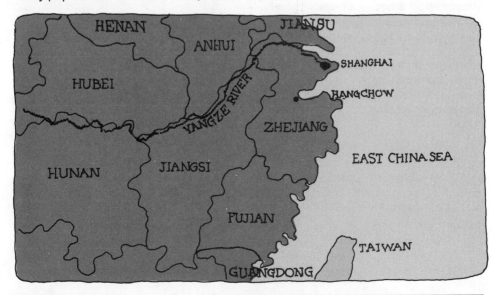

49

Steamed Chicken with Ham and Broccoli

Preparation Time: 40 minutes
Cooking Time: 20 minutes
Cooking Technique: Steaming

5 cups chicken broth
3 scallions
1 slice ginger root, ¼-inch thick
1 clove garlic
3 whole chicken breasts,
   skinned and boned
1 bunch (1 pound) broccoli

1 tablespoon soy sauce
½ teaspoon brown sugar
⅓ cup cornstarch
1 tablespoon dry white wine
   or dry sherry
¼ pound sliced boiled ham,
   cut in 1-inch pieces

Place 2½ cups chicken broth, scallions, ginger root and garlic in the wok. Place steamer insert or rack in wok and put chicken on rack. Separate broccoli into florets and cut stems into ½-inch slices. Arrange broccoli on top of chicken. Cover. Set heat control dial at 250° F. Steam for 12 to 15 minutes or until broccoli is tender and juices of chicken run clear. While chicken and broccoli are cooking, add all the remaining ingredients except ham to the remaining chicken broth. Remove and reserve chicken and broccoli. Remove steamer insert, discard scallions, ginger root and garlic. Pour combined broth ingredients into wok. Set heat control dial at 275° F., simmer stirring occasionally until sauce thickens, about 5 minutes. While sauce is simmering, cut chicken into 1-inch pieces. Return chicken, broccoli and ham to wok. Stir well to combine. Heat until hot, about 1 minute. Serve immediately over rice.

Makes: 4 to 6 servings

Deep-fried Shrimp and Rice Balls

Preparation time: 5 minutes
Cookingtime:10 minutes
Cooking technique: Deep-frying

¾ pound shrimp, cooked and cleaned
6 water chestnuts
¼ pound mushrooms
½ cup cooked rice
1 egg

1 teaspoon sesame oil
2 teaspoons soy sauce
3 cups vegetable oil
2 tablespoons cornstarch

In a food processor or blender chop all ingredients except cornstarch and vegetable oil. Pour oil into wok. Set heat control dial at 425° F. While oil is heating, form mixture into 24 (1-inch) balls. Dredge in cornstarch, shaking off excess. When light goes out deep-fry shrimp balls for 5 minutes or until lightly browned. Drain on tempura rack or absorbent paper towels. Serve hot with duck sauce or cocktail sauce for dipping.

Makes: 24

Red-cooked Chicken

Preparation time: 5 minutes
Cooking time: 1 hour 30 minutes
Cooking technique: Red-stewing

3 cups water
2 cups soy sauce
1 clove garlic

1 slice ginger root, ½-inch thick
1 star anise, or 1 teaspoon anise
   extract
1 chicken (2½ to 3 pounds), whole

Place all ingredients in wok. Set heat control dial at 250° F. Cover. Simmer for 1 hour 30 minutes. Turn chicken every half hour. Cut into serving pieces and serve with stir-fried vegetables and rice.

Makes: 4 servings

Lion's Head

Preparation time: 20 minutes
Cooking time: 20 minutes
Cooking technique: Shallow-frying, Steaming

½ cup vegetable oil
½ pound ground beef
½ pound ground pork
2 scallions, finely chopped
6 water chestnuts, finely chopped
3 mushrooms, finely chopped
1 egg
2 tablespoons cornstarch
2 tablespoons soy sauce

2 teaspoons sesame oil
2 cups chicken broth
¼ cup soy sauce
2 tablespoons cornstarch
1 teaspoon sugar
⅛ teaspoon pepper
1 pound Chinese cabbage, angle-cut
   in 2-inch pieces

Pour oil into wok. Set heat control dial at 350° F. While oil is heating combine beef, pork, scallions, water chestnuts, mushrooms, egg, cornstarch, soy sauce and sesame oil. Form into 8 (2½-inch) meatballs. When light goes out place meatballs in wok carefully. Shallow-fry until browned on all sides, about 5 mintues. Remove and re-serve. Carefully discard oil. Wipe wok clean with paper towel. Combine remaining ingredients and pour mixture into wok. Simmer, stirring constantly until mixture thickens, about 1 minute. Return meatballs to wok. Place cabbage on top of meatballs. Turn heat control dial to 250° F. Cover. Steam for 15 minutes.

Makes: 6 servings

Red-cooked Beef

Preparation time: 5 minutes
Cooking time: 2½ hours
Cooking technique: Red-stewing

2 tablespoons vegetable oil
1 clove garlic, mashed
1 slice ginger root, cut ¼-inch thick
3 scallions, chopped
1 beef roast (4 pounds)
1 star anise or ½ teaspoon Chinese
   five spice powder

½ cup soy sauce
¼ cup dry white wine
   or dry sherry
2 cups water
1 tablespoon brown sugar
½ teaspoon sesame oil
½ teaspoon crushed red pepper

Pour oil into wok. Set heat control dial at 350° F. When light goes out add garlic, ginger root and scallions. Stir-fry 1 minute. Remove and reserve. Add beef roast and brown well on all sides, about 10 minutes. Combine remaining ingredients. Pour mixture into wok. Add reserved garlic, ginger root and scallions. Cover. Turn heat control dial to 250° F. Simmer for 2½ hours or until tender. Strain liquid. Cut beef into thin slices and serve with juices. As an alternative, slice into 2-inch strips. Chill. Pour liquid into 8 x 8 x 2-inch pan. Chill. Allow to jell. Cube jelly and serve with meat.

Makes: 8 main dish servings or 16 hors d'oeuvres servings

Deep-fried Chinese Lemon Drop Cakes

Preparation time: 15 minutes
Cooking time: 5 minutes
Cooking technique: Deep-frying

3 cups vegetable oil
2 tablespoons butter
1 cup sugar
1 egg

1 teaspoon lemon extract
2 cups all-purpose flour
2 teaspoons baking powder
⅓ to ½ cup water
confectioners' sugar

Pour oil into wok. Set heat control dial at 425° F. While oil is heating beat butter and sugar in a large bowl, until combined. Add egg and extract and beat until fluffy. Stir in flour and baking powder. Add water a little at a time. Use just enough to be able to form dough into a ball. Divide dough into 24 equal pieces. Moisten your hands and form pieces into small balls. When light goes out add dough and deep fry until well browned, about 3 minutes. Drain on tempura rack or absorbent paper towels. Allow to cool and sprinkle with confectioners' sugar.

Makes: 24

Shanghai-style Egg *Fu Yung*

Preparation time: 5 minutes
Cooking time: 3 minutes
Cooking technique: Stir-frying

4 egg whites
¼ cup milk
¼ pound cooked shrimp, chopped
3 scallions, minced

¼ teaspoon salt
Pinch pepper
1 tablespoon vegetable oil

In a large bowl beat egg whites with an electric mixer until they form soft peaks. In a small bowl combine remaining ingredients except oil. Pour oil into wok. Set heat control dial at 300° F. While oil is heating gently fold shrimp mixture into egg whites. When light goes out pour mixture into wok. Stir constantly until dry, about 1 minute. Do not allow eggs to brown.

Makes: 2 to 3 servings.

Red Wine Sediment Paste

Preparation time: 5 minutes
Cooking time: 15 minutes
Cooking technique: Simmering

½ cup red wine
2 tablespoons catsup
½ teaspoon powdered ginger
3 pieces dried spicy bean curd
2 tablespoons brown sugar
1 clove garlic, minced

2 tablespoons orange juice
1 tablespoon all-purpose flour
1 teaspoon soy sauce
½ teaspoon grated orange peel
¼ teaspoon Chinese five spice
   powder

Place all ingredients into wok. Stir well to combine. Set heat control dial at 225° F. Cover. Simmer for 15 minutes. Cool. Store in clean covered jar in refrigerator for use as needed.

Makes: ¾ cup

Chicken with Red Wine Sediment Paste

Preparation time: 5 minutes
Marinating time: 30 minutes
Cooking time: 35 minutes
Cooking technique: Stir-frying, Simmering

MARINADE:

2 tablespoons Red Wine Sediment
   Paste
1 tablespoon soy sauce
1 tablespoon white wine

½ teaspoon sesame oil
2 teaspoons brown sugar
½ cup chicken broth

1 chicken (2½ to 3 pounds) cut
   in pieces
2 tablespoons vegetable oil
1 clove garlic, mashed

1 medium onion, cut in strips
1 can (6 ounces) water chestnuts,
   drained and sliced

In a large bowl, combine marinade. Place chicken in bowl and marinate ½ hour. Pour oil into wok. Set heat control dial at 350° F. When light goes out add garlic and stir-fry 1 minute. Remove and discard. Add onion and water chestnuts and stir-fry 2 minutes. Push up sides of wok. Remove chicken from marinade. Reserve marinade. Add chicken and stir-fry until lightly browned, about 10 minutes. Stir in onions and water chestnuts. Add marinade. Turn heat control dial to 250° F. Cover. Simmer 20 minutes. Serve with rice.

Makes: 4 to 6 servings

Miniature Corn and Straw Mushrooms

Preparation time: 5 minutes
Cooking time: 5 minutes
Cooking technique: Stir-frying, Simmering

2 tablespoons vegetable oil
1 medium onion, cut in strips
1 clove garlic, minced
1 can (6½ ounces) bamboo shoots,
   drained
1 can (15 ounces) miniature corn,
   drained
1 can (15 ounces) straw mushrooms,
   drained

1 cup chicken broth
¼ cup red wine sediment paste
2 teaspoons brown sugar
2 teaspoons cornstarch
2 tablespoons white wine
2 tablespoons soy sauce
½ teaspoon sesame seed oil

Pour oil into wok. Set heat control dial at 350° F. When light goes out add onion and stir-fry 2 minutes. Add garlic and stir-fry 30 seconds. Push up sides of wok. Add bamboo shoots and corn and stir-fry 1 minute. Push up sides of wok. Add mushrooms, stir-fry 1 minute and push up sides of wok. Combine remaining ingredients and pour mixture into wok. Simmer, stirring constantly until mixture thickens, about 1 minute. Stir in vegetables from side of wok and heat until hot, about 1 minute. Serve immediately.

Makes: 6 servings

Twice-cooked Duck with Vegetables

Preparation time: l5 minutes
Cooking time: 1 hour
Cooking technique: Steaming, Deep-frying, Stir-frying

2 cups water
1 duck (5 pounds) cut in quarters
3 cups vegetable oil
½ cup cornstarch
1 clove garlic, mashed

1 slice ginger root, cut ¼-inch thick
3 carrots, roll-cut in
   ½-inch pieces
2 onions, cut in ¼-inch wedges
1 can (8 ounces) water chestnuts,
   drained and sliced

SAUCE:
¼ cup soy sauce
½ cup orange juice
⅓ cup Plum Sauce
½ cup water

⅓ cup Sweet and Sour
   Sauce or duck sauce
1 teaspoon hoisin sauce

Pour water into wok. Place steamer insert or rack into wok. Remove as much fat as possible from duck and place duck on rack. Cover. Set heat control dial at 250° F. Steam for 40 minutes. Prick skin of duck with a fork twice during steaming. Remove duck from wok. Remove bones from breast section and cut meat into bite-size pieces. Leave legs and wings whole. Reserve. Remove steamer rack and discard water. Rinse out wok and dry well. Pour oil into wok. Set heat control dial at 425° F. While oil is heating dredge duck in cornstarch. Shake off excess. When light goes out add duck and deep-fry until golden brown, about 10 minutes. Drain on tempura rack or absorbent paper towels. Carefully remove all but 2 tablespoons oil with a long handled ladle. Set heat control dial at 350° F. and when light goes out add garlic and ginger root. Stir-fry 1 minute and discard. Add carrots and stir-fry 3 minutes. Push up sides of wok. Add onions and stir-fry 2 minutes. Push up sides of wok. Add water chestnuts and stir-fry 1 minute. Combine sauce ingredients. Brush duck with sauce mixture. Stir in all vegetables from sides of wok. Add duck and heat 1 minute. Serve immediately with rice and remaining sauce.

Makes: 4 servings

Savory Leg of Lamb

Preparation time: 10 minutes
Cooking time: 2 hours 20 minutes
Cooking technique: Red-stewing

2 tablespoons vegetable oil
3 cloves garlic, minced
1 slice ginger root,
   cut ¼-inch thick
1 medium onion, cut in strips
½ leg of lamb (3½ pounds)
¾ cup soy sauce

2 tablespoons wine
2 teaspoons brown sugar
¼ teaspoon Chinese five spice
   powder
2 cups water
1 cup chicken broth
2 teaspoons cornstarch
½ cup water

Pour oil into wok. Set heat control dial at 350° F. When light goes out stir-fry ginger and garlic 1 minute. Push up sides of wok. Stir-fry onions 3 minutes, push up sides of wok. Add lamb and brown until well browned on all sides, about 20 minutes. Combine soy sauce, wine, sugar, spice powder, water and broth. Pour into wok. Turn heat control dial to 250° F. Cover. Simmer for 2 hours. Combine cornstarch and water. Remove lamb and cut into slices. Pour cornstarch mixture into wok stirring constantly until sauce thickens, about 1 minute. Return lamb to wok and heat 2 minutes or until hot. Serve immediately.

Makes: 6 to 8 servings

Steamed Fish Steaks with Dried Black Mushrooms

Preparation time: 10 minutes
Cooking time: 15 minutes
Cooking technique: Steaming, Stir-frying

6 Chinese dried black mushrooms
3 cups water
3 cod steaks (about ½ pound each)
1 teaspoon salt
¼ teaspoon pepper
3 strips bacon, cut in 1-inch pieces
4 scallions, chopped

1 can (6 ounces) water chestnuts,
   drained and sliced
1 clove garlic, minced
½ cup chicken stock
2 tablespoons vinegar
2 tablespoons soy sauce
1½ teaspoons cornstarch

Soak mushrooms for 15 minutes in a small amount of water. Drain and reserve. Pour 3 cups water into wok. Place steamer rack into wok. Place fish on rack and sprinkle with salt and pepper. Cover. Set heat control dial to 250° F. Steam until fish flakes easily with a fork, about 5 to 8 minutes. Remove fish to a platter and cover with aluminum foil. Discard water. Wipe wok clean with paper towel. Turn heat control dial to 350° F. When light goes out add bacon to wok and fry until crisp. Push up sides of wok. Add scallions, water chestnuts, garlic and mushrooms and stir-fry 1 minute. Remove and reserve. Combine remaining ingredients. Pour mixture into wok and simmer, stirring constantly until the mixture thickens, about 1 minute. Return bacon and vegetables to wok. Heat until hot, about 2 minutes. Pour vegetables and sauce over fish steaks. Serve immediately.

Makes: 4 servings

Tofu with Vegetables

Preparation time: 20 minutes
Cooking time: 10 minutes
Cooking technique: Stir-frying

¼ cup vegetable oil
1 clove garlic, mashed
1 can (8 ounces) water chestnuts,
   drained and sliced
2 carrots, angle-cut into thin slices
3 stalks celery, angle-cut into
   thin slices
1 medium onion, cut in strips
¼ pound snow peas

¼ pound Chinese cabbage, chopped
½ pound firm style *tofu*, cut in
   thin slices
½ cup beef broth
2 teaspoons cornstarch
1 teaspoon salt
1 teaspoon sugar
¼ teaspoon pepper

Pour 2 tablespoons oil into wok. Set heat control dial at 350° F. When light goes out add garlic and stir-fry 1 minute. Remove and discard. Add water chestnuts and carrots and stir-fry 2 minutes. Push up sides of wok. Add celery and onion and stir-fry 2 minutes. Push up sides of wok. Add snow peas and stir-fry 1 minute. Push up sides of wok. Add remaining oil and when light goes out add Chinese cabbage and stir-fry 1 minute. Push up sides of wok. Add *tofu* and stir-fry 1 minute. Combine remaining ingredients and pour mixture into wok. Simmer, stirring constantly until mixture thickens, about 1 minute. Return all ingredients to wok. Stir well to combine. Heat until hot, about 1 minute. Serve immediately.

Makes: 6 servings

Western China — Szechuan Province

Much of the western region of China is so mountainous it is uninhabitable. The Red Basin of Szechuan, however, is very heavily populated. The land is very fertile and agriculture is intense even though only a small percentage of the land is flat. The more hilly areas are terraced heavily for full use.

The climate is tropical and there is abundant rain and very little chance of freezing temperatures. The summers are hot and humid and the winters are cold and damp. The main crops are those generally typical for warm areas, rice, sugar cane and citrus fruits. Tea, wheat, corn and potatoes are also grown on the steep hills and lower mountains

The most striking thing about the cooking of the region is the liberal use of hot pepper. If you are tasting Szechuan cooking for the first time, be prepared! You will also often find a variety of flavors in one dish, hot, sour and salty, for example, as in Szechuan cabbage.

The stir-frying of this region is a little different from Cantonese. Here, less sauce is prepared so there is not as much gravy surrounding the meats and vegetables.

The texture of the food is also emphasized, and the food goes from deliberately chewy to silky smooth. The use of multiple cooking processes is also liberally employed. It is not unusual for meats to be steamed or stewed and then stir-fried or deep-fried.

Yunnan is located to the south of Szechuan. The cooking of this province is influenced by Szechuan as well as Burma and India. You will find the heavy use of curries and other hot spices as well as delicious ham dishes.

Hunan province, which borders Szechuan on the East is well known for excellent glutinous rice which is a short grain rice that is very sticky when cooked.

Although many of the recipes in this section are quite spicy they were toned down a bit to suit more moderate tastes. Be prudent in your use of the peppers called for, you can always add more to suit your taste. There are a lot of interesting recipes here which offer a contrast to the milder ones found throughout the rest of this book.

Honey Chicken

Preparation time: 5 minutes
Cooking time: 40 minutes
Cooking technique: Shallow-frying, Steaming

¼ cup vegetable oil
1 clove garlic, mashed
1 slice ginger root, cut ¼-inch thick
1 chicken (2½ to 3 pounds),
   cut in pieces

¼ cup soy sauce
¼ cup white wine
¼ cup honey
¼ teaspoon garlic salt

Pour oil into wok. Set heat control dial at 350° F. When light goes out add garlic and ginger root, stir-fry 1 minute. Remove and discard. Add chicken, shallow-fry until well browned on all sides, about 15 minutes. While chicken is browning, combine remaining ingredients. Remove chicken. Discard oil. Wipe wok clean with a paper towel. Pour mixure into wok. Return chicken. Stir well to coat chicken. Turn heat control dial to 250° F. Simmer for 20 minutes. Turn after first 10 minutes. Remove chicken to serving platter and spoon sauce over all.

Makes: 4 to 6 servings

Pork and Eggplant Stir-fry

Preparation time: 15 minutes
Marinating time: 1 hour
Cooking time: 15 minutes
Cooking technique: Stir-frying

MARINADE:
1 clove garlic, minced
¼ teaspoon powdered ginger
¼ cup soy sauce

½ cup water
2 teaspoons brown sugar
1 tablespoon cornstarch

1 pound boneless pork,
   cut in 1-inch cubes
1 eggplant (1 pound),
   cut in 1-inch cubes

1 tablespoon cornstarch
⅓ cup vegetable oil
1 medium onion, cut in strips

In a large bowl combine the marinade ingredients. Add pork and marinate for 1 hour. While pork is marinating prepare remaining ingredients. Dredge eggplant in cornstarch, shaking off excess. Pour 2 tablespoons oil into wok. Set heat control dial at 350° F. Drain pork on absorbent paper towels. Reserve marinade. When light goes out add pork and stir-fry 8 to 10 minutes. Push up sides of wok. Add onions and stir-fry 2 minutes. Remove pork and onions and reserve. Add remaining oil. When light goes out add eggplant and stir-fry 2 minutes. Remove and reserve. Pour reserved marinade into wok. Simmer, stirring constantly until mixture thickens, about 1 minute. Return all ingredients to wok. Stir well to combine. Heat until hot, about 1 minute.

Makes: 4 servings

Szechuan Cabbage

Preparation time: 15 minutes
Cooking time: 5 minutes
Cooking technique: Stir-frying

¼ cup vegetable oil
1 pound Chinese cabbage, angle-cut
   into 1-inch pieces
3 cloves garlic, minced

½ teaspoon Sichuan pepper corns
1 teaspoon crushed red pepper
1 teaspoon salt
1 tablespoon white vinegar

Pour oil into wok. Set heat control dial at 350° F. Add cabbage and stir-fry 3 minutes. Stir in remaining ingredients and stir-fry 1 minute. Serve immediately.

Makes: 4 servings

Tofu with Chicken and Mushrooms

Preparation time: 10 minutes
Cooking time: 15 minutes
Cooking technique: Deep-frying, Stir-frying

---

1 tablespoon cloud ear mushrooms
3 cups vegetable oil
1 pound *tofu*, firm style, cut
   in 1-inch cubes
2 whole chicken breasts, skinned,
   boned and cut in 1-inch pieces
1 clove garlic, mashed
1 slice ginger root
1 onion, cut into shreds

¼ teaspoon fermented black beans,
   minced
1 can (8 ounces) sliced bamboo
   shoots, drained
1½ cups chicken broth
½ to 1 teaspoon crushed red pepper
2 tablespoons cornstarch
2 tablespoons dry white wine or
   dry sherry
1 teaspoon sugar

Soak mushrooms in a small amount of water for about 30 minutes. Drain and reserve. Pour oil into wok. Set heat control dial at 425° F. When light goes out carefully add *tofu* and deep-fry until lightly browned, about 5 minutes. Remove and drain on tempura rack or absorbent paper towels. Add chicken and deep-fry until well browned, about 3 to 5 minutes. Drain all but 2 tablespoons of oil from wok. Turn heat control dial to 350° F. When light goes out add garlic and ginger root and stir-fry 1 minute. Remove and discard. Add onions and stir-fry 2 minutes. Push up sides of wok. Add black beans and stir-fry 30 seconds. Push up sides of wok. Add bamboo shoots and reserved mushrooms and stir-fry 1 minute. Push up sides of wok. Combine remaining ingredients and pour into wok. Simmer, stirring constantly until mixture thickens, about 1 minute. Stir in all ingredients from sides of wok. Return chicken and *tofu*. Stir gently to combine. Heat until hot, about 2 minutes.

Makes: 6 servings

Stir-fry Chicken with Spinach

Preparation time: 10 minutes
Marinating time: 1 hour
Cooking time: 10 minutes
Cooking technique: Stir-frying, Steaming

MARINADE:

1½ cups chicken broth
1 tablespoon cornstarch
2 tablespoons soy sauce
2 tablespoons dry white wine
   or dry sherry

1 teaspoon brown sugar
⅛ teaspoon powdered ginger
⅛ teaspoon Chinese five spice
   powder

1 pound boneless chicken breasts,
   cut in 1-inch cubes
¼ cup vegetable oil
1 clove garlic
1 slice ginger root, cut ¼-inch thick

3 scallions, sliced
6 water chestnuts, sliced
1 can (8½ ounces) sliced bamboo
   shoots, drained
4 cups spinach, cleaned

In a large bowl combine marinade ingredients. Marinate chicken for 1 hour. Pour oil into wok. Set heat control dial at 350° F. When light goes out add garlic and ginger root and stir-fry 1 minute. Remove and discard. Add scallions, water chestnuts and bamboo shoots. Stir-fry 2 minutes. Remove and reserve. Add chicken and stir-fry 3 minutes. Remove and reserve. Pour marinade into wok. Stir constantly until mixture thickens, about 1 minute. Return all ingredients to wok. Stir to combine. Place spinach on top of mixture. Cover. Turn heat control dial to 250° F. and steam until spinach is limp, about 5 minutes.

Makes: 4 servings

Spicy Eggplant

Preparation time: 10 minutes
Cooking time: 10 minutes
Cooking technique: Stir-frying, Simmering

⅓ cup vegetable oil
1 eggplant (1 pound),
   cut in 1-inch cubes
1 tablespoon chili powder
1 tablespoon soy sauce
1 tablespoon vinegar

1 teaspoon brown sugar
1 teaspoon garlic salt
2 tablespoons dry white
   wine
1 cup chicken broth

Pour oil into wok. Set heat control dial at 350° F. When light goes out add eggplant and stir-fry 5 minutes. Add remaining ingredients and stir well. Turn heat control to 250° F. Cover and simmer 3 minutes.

Makes: 4 to 6 servings.

Twice-cooked Pork Szechuan

Preparation time: 5 minutes
Cooking time: 1 hour 15 minutes
Cooking technique: Red-stewing, Stir-frying

2 cups water
1 pound boneless pork roast
2 cloves garlic, crushed
1 slice ginger root, cut ¼-inch thick
1½ cups soy sauce
3½ cups water
2 tablespoons brown sugar
2 tablespoons dry white wine or
    dry sherry

3 tablespoons vegetable oil
½ cup water
2 teaspoons cornstarch
2 teaspoons hoisin sauce
½ teaspoon crushed red pepper
1 clove garlic, mashed
1 slice ginger root, cut ¼-inch thick
3 scallions, chopped

Pour water into wok. Set heat control dial at 250° F. When water boils add pork. Cover and cook for 10 minutes. While pork is cooking combine garlic, ginger, soy sauce, water, brown sugar and wine. Remove pork from wok, discard water and wipe wok clean. Pour combined mixture into wok and return defatted pork. Cover. Set heat control dial at 250° F. and simmer for 1 hour. Remove pork from stewing liquid. Cool. Slice pork into 1-inch thick slices. Reserve 1 cup of liquid and combine with ½ cup water, cornstarch, hoisin sauce and red pepper. Discard remaining liquid. Wipe wok with paper towel. Pour oil into wok. Set heat control dial at 350° F. When light goes out add garlic and ginger root. Stir-fry 1 minute. Remove and discard. Add scallions and stir-fry 1 minute. Push up sides of wok. Add sliced meat and stir-fry 1 minute. Push up sides of wok. Pour reserved liquid into wok. Simmer, stirring constantly until mixture thickens, about 1 minute. Stir in meat and scallions from sides of wok and heat 1 minute. Serve immediately.

Makes: 4 servings

Pork Dumpling Soup

Preparation time: 30 minutes
Cooking time: 30 minutes
Cooking technique: Simmering

2 cups all-purpose flour
⅔ cup boiling water
¼ cup cold water

FILLING:

½ pound ground pork
2 scallions, chopped
2 mushrooms, minced
½ cup finely chopped Chinese
   cabbage
6 water chestnuts, minced

2 tablespoons soy sauce
1 egg
½ teaspoon sesame oil
1 teaspoon cornstarch
1 teaspoon salt
¼ teaspoon pepper

6 cups chicken broth

In a large bowl combine flour and hot and cold water. With lightly floured hands knead well to form a soft ball. Cover. Allow to stand for 15 minutes. While dough is standing, combine filling ingredients. Pour broth into wok. Set heat control dial at 250° F. While broth is heating roll out dough as thin as possible on a lightly floured board. Cut into 24 three-inch rounds with a biscuit cutter or the top of a glass. Spoon about 1 heaping teaspoon full of filling in center of each round. Fold over and crimp edges with a fork to seal. When broth boils carefully drop half of the dumplings into the wok. Boil for 15 minutes. Place in a serving bowl. Add remaining dumplings to wok and boil for 15 minutes. Return all dumplings to wok and heat for 2 minutes. Pour dumplings and broth into serving bowl. Serve as a soup.

Makes: 6 to 8 servings

Scallops with Snow Peas and Black Bean Sauce

Preparation time: 10 minutes
Cooking time: 5 minutes
Cooking technique: Stir-frying

¼ cup vegetable oil
2 cloves garlic, mashed
1 slice ginger root, cut ¼-inch thick
3 scallions, sliced
1 pound bay scallops*
6 mushrooms, sliced
¼ pound snow peas

1 cup chicken broth
1 tablespoon cornstarch
2 tablespoons soy sauce
2 tablespoons dry white wine
1 tablespoon fermented black beans, chopped
1 teaspoon brown sugar

Pour 2 tablespoons oil into wok. Set heat control dial at 350° F. When light goes out stir-fry garlic and ginger root for 1 minute. Remove and discard. Add scallions and stir-fry 2 minutes. Push up sides of wok. Add scallops and stir-fry until tender, 2 to 5 minutes. Add remaining oil as needed. When light goes out add mushrooms and snow peas and stir-fry 1 minute. Push up sides of wok. Combine remaining ingredients and stir into wok, stirring constantly until mixture thickens, about 1 minute. Stir in scallops and vegetables to coat well. Serve immediately.

Makes: 4 servings

* Bay scallops are very small. If they are not available, cut scallops into ½-inch pieces.

Szechuan Shrimp

Preparation time: 30 minutes
Marinating time: 20 minutes
Cooking time: 10 minutes
Cooking technique: Stir-frying

MARINADE:
1 tablespoon soy sauce
2 tablespoons catsup
1 clove garlic, minced

½ to 1 teaspoon dried crushed red pepper
½ teaspoon cornstarch

1 pound shrimp, cleaned, shelled and deveined
2 tablespoons vegetable oil
1 clove garlic, crushed

1 slice ginger root, cut ¼-inch thick
4 scallions, minced
1 can (6 ounces) water chestnuts drained and sliced

In a large bowl combine marinade ingredients. Add shrimp and marinate 20 minutes. Pour oil into wok. Set heat control dial at 350° F. When light goes out add garlic and ginger root and stir-fry 1 minute. Remove and discard. Add scallions and water chestnuts and stir-fry 2 minutes. Leave in wok. Add shrimp to wok and stir-fry until shrimp are tender, about 3 to 5 minutes. Serve with rice.

Makes 4 servings

Pearl Balls

Preparation time: 15 minutes
Soaking time: 2 to 3 hours
Cooking time: 10 minutes
Cooking technique: Steaming

1 cup glutinous rice
1 clove garlic, minced
½ slice ginger, finely minced
3 scallions, minced
¼ pound ground pork
1 pound ground beef
½ cup chopped Chinese cabbage

3 mushrooms, finely chopped
½ teaspoon hoisin sauce
2 teaspoons Sweet and Sour Sauce
1 teaspoon dry white wine
1 teaspoon salt
½ teaspoon crushed red pepper
2 cups water

Soak rice for 2 to 3 hours. Combine all ingredients except rice and water. Form into 45 (1-inch) balls. Drain rice and roll meatballs in rice. Place steamer insert or rack into wok. Pour water into wok. Place pearl balls on rack. Cover. Set heat control dial at 250° F. Steam for 10 minutes. Serve with Mustard Sauce (page 23) or Plum Sauce (page 22).

Makes: 45

Peppery Meatballs with Mustard Sauce

Preparation time: 10 minutes
Cooking time: 10 minutes
Cooking technique: Shallow-frying

½ cup vegetable oil
½ pound ground pork
¼ pound ground beef
2 mushrooms, finely chopped
1 clove garlic, minced
2 tablespoons chopped Chinese
    cabbage

1 tablespoon cornstarch
¼ to ½ teaspoon crushed red pepper
2 tablespoons soy sauce
1 teaspoon sesame seeds
1 egg

Pour oil into wok. Set heat control dial at 350° F. In a large bowl combine all remaining ingredients. Form mixture into 36 (½-inch) meatballs. When light goes out shallow fry until very well browned on all sides, about 10 minutes. Serve as an hors d'oeuvres with Mustard Sauce (page 23) and/or Sweet and Sour Sauce (page 23).

Makes: 36

Braised Spareribs

Preparation time: 10 minutes
Cooking time: 40 minutes
Cooking technique: Stir-frying, Braising

2 tablespoons vegetable oil
1 rack (2½ to 3½ pounds) pork
    spare ribs, cut into individual ribs
1 clove garlic, minced
3 scallions, chopped
¼ teaspoon fermented black beans,
    chopped

¼ teaspoon powdered ginger
2 tablespoons soy sauce
½ cup chicken stock or broth
2 tablespoons honey

Pour oil into wok. Set heat control dial at 350° F. When light goes out add one-third of the spare ribs and brown well on both sides, about 6 to 8 minutes. Continue until all ribs are browned. Remove and reserve. Add garlic, scallions and black beans and stir-fry 1 minute. Add remaining ingredients and stir well to combine. Return ribs to wok and toss well to coat. Turn heat control dial to 275° F. Cover and braise for 30 minutes, turning once after 15 minutes.

Makes: 4 servings

Chinese-American

There are many recipes that are really not classic Chinese but actually Chinese-American. The most famous example is Chop Suey. As the story goes, one night in the home of the Chinese Ambassador to Washington, Li Hung Chang, unexpected guests dropped in. The envoy called to his cook for something to eat. To the cook's horror the cupboard was virtually bare. He used his imagination and put together a delicious dish that was a combination of bits and pieces of foods that he had on hand. Thus the birth of the famous dish, originally known as Li Hung Chang Chop Suey. It is actually a variation of a classic Chinese dish, *Sub Gum. Sub Gum* means "many precious things" and is a combination dish which usually includes several types of meat and vegetables.

Most Chinese-American recipes have their basis in the classic cuisine of China. They have been altered in various ways over the years, probably due simply to availability of ingredients and the whims of the chefs. Most of the more well known are based on Cantonese recipes. The following selection includes hors d'oeuvres, as well as main dishes.

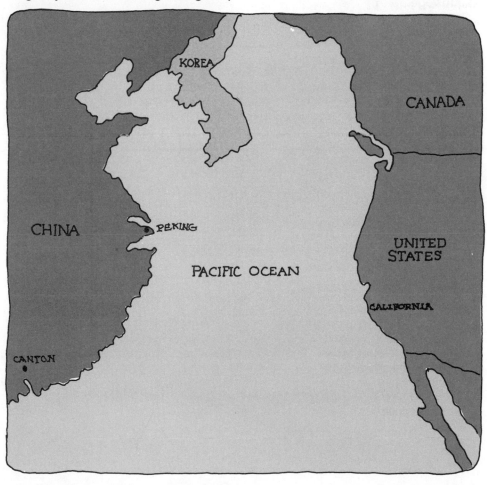

Potstickers -*Guotie*

Preparation time: 20 minutes
Cooking time: 25 minutes
Cooking technique: Shallow-frying, Simmering

DUMPLINGS:
3 cups all-purpose flour
½ teaspoon salt
1¼ cups water

FILLING:
½ pound ground beef
¼ pound ground pork
½ cup chopped Chinese cabbage
4 scallions, finely chopped
½ cup vegetable oil

1 clove garlic, minced
4 mushrooms, finely chopped
2 tablespoons soy sauce
½ teaspoon sesame oil

3 cups beef broth
Chili Dipping Sauce

In a large bowl, combine flour, salt and water. With lightly floured hands, knead well to form a soft ball, about 3 minutes. Cover with a damp cloth and allow to stand for 30 minutes. While dough is standing, prepare filling by combining all ingredients. Roll out dough as thin as possible. Cut into 36 (3-inch) circles with a biscuit cutter or the top of a glass. Pour oil into wok. Set heat control dial at 350° F. While oil is heating spoon about 2 teaspoons of filling in the center of each dough round. Fold over and crimp edges together with a fork to seal. When light goes out, add about ¼ of the dumplings to the wok and shallow-fry until well browned, about 3 to 5 minutes per side. Drain on tempura rack or absorbent paper towels. When all potstickers are fried, turn heat control dial to "off." Remove potstickers with a slotted spoon to a serving platter. Carefully discard oil. Wipe wok clean with a paper towel. Pour broth into wok, set heat control dial at 225° F. Add potstickers, cover and simmer 10 minutes. Serve hot with Chili Dipping Sauce. Fill small teacups with broth to drink.

Makes: About 36 dumplings

Chili Dipping Sauce

½ cup soy sauce
½ cup beef consommé
¼ cup sesame or salad oil

2 tablespoons vinegar
1 teaspoon hot pepper
   sauce

Blend all ingredients and serve in individual dipping cups with potstickers.

Makes: 1⅓ cups

Sub Gum Fried Rice

Preparation time: 20 minutes
Cooking time: 10 minutes
Cooking technique: Stir-frying

¼ cup vegetable oil
2 eggs, well beaten
1 medium onion, cut in strips
½ chicken breast, skinned, boned
   and cut in thin shreds
¼ pound ham, cut in thin shreds

4 mushrooms, chopped
½ cup bean sprouts
½ cup peas
3 cups cooked rice
½ cup soy sauce

Pour 2 teaspoons oil into wok. Set heat control dial at 250° F. When light goes out pour eggs into wok. Do not stir; allow eggs to set. When cooked, remove and cut into ¼-inch shreds. Pour 2 tablespoons oil into wok. Set heat control dial at 350° F. When light goes out add onions and stir-fry 2 minutes. Push up sides of wok. Add chicken and ham, stir-fry 2 minutes. Remove and reserve onions and meats. Add oil if needed. When light goes out add mushrooms, bean sprouts and peas. Stir-fry 30 seconds. Remove and reserve. Stir-fry rice 1 minute. Return all reserved ingredients to wok. Add soy sauce. Stir to combine. Serve immediately.

Makes: 6 servings

Beef *Chop Suey*

Preparation time: 20 minutes
Cooking time: 10 minutes
Cooking technique: Stir-frying

¼ cup vegetable oil
1 clove garlic
1 slice ginger root, cut ¼-inch thick
4 stalks celery, cut in 1-inch
   long thin strips
1 can (8 ounces) water chestnuts,
   drained and sliced
4 scallions, cut in thin strips

1 pound flank steak, angle-cut
   in thin stips
1 cup bean sprouts
1 cup beef broth
2 tablespoons dry white wine or
   dry sherry
2 tablespoons soy sauce
½ teaspoon brown sugar
1 tablespoon cornstarch

Pour 2 tablespoons oil in wok. Set heat control dial at 350° F. When light goes out add garlic and ginger root. Stir-fry 1 minute. Remove and discard. Add celery and stir-fry 1 minute. Remove and reserve. Add water chestnuts and scallions and stir-fry 2 minutes. Add remaining oil. When light goes out add steak and stir-fry 2 minutes. Remove and reserve. Combine remaining ingredients and pour mixture into wok. Simmer, stirring constantly, until mixture thickens, about 1 minute. Return all ingredients to wok. Stir well to combine. Heat until hot, about 1 minute. Serve immediately.

Makes: 4 servings

Shrimp with Broccoli and Croutons

Preparation time: 20 minutes
Marinating time: 15 minutes
Cooking time: 20 minutes
Cooking technique: Steaming, Stir-frying

1 pound shrimp, shelled
  and deveined
2 tablespoons soy sauce

1 tablespoon dry white wine or
  dry sherry

2 cups water
1 bunch (1 pound) broccoli
2 tablespoons vegetable oil
1 clove garlic, mashed
1 slice ginger root, cut
  ¼-inch thick
3 scallions

2 tablespoons dry white wine or
  dry sherry
2 tablespoons oyster sauce
2 teaspoons brown sugar
1 cup chicken broth
1 tablespoon cornstarch
1 cup flavored croutons

In a small bowl marinate shrimp in soy sauce and wine for 15 minutes. While shrimp is marinating place steamer insert or rack in wok. Pour water into wok. Put broccoli on insert. Cover. Set heat control dial at 250° F. Steam for 10 to 12 minutes. Remove broccoli and insert. Wipe wok clean with paper towels. Pour oil into wok. Set heat control dial at 350° F. When light goes out add garlic, ginger root, scallions and stir-fry 1 minute. Remove and discard. Add marinated shrimp and stir-fry for 3 to 5 minutes. Remove and reserve. Combine remaining ingredients except croutons and pour into wok. Simmer, stirring constantly until mixture thickens, about 1 minute. Return all ingredients to wok. Stir well to combine. Heat until hot, about 1 minute. Top with croutons.

Makes: 4 servings

Shrimp and Green Beans

Preparation time: 15 minutes
Cooking time: 10 minutes
Cooking technique: Stir-frying

2 tablespoons vegetable oil
1 clove garlic, minced
4 scallions, thinly sliced
¼ pound green beans, angle-cut into
 ¼-inch pieces
1 pound raw shrimp, peeled and
 deveined

1 can (8 ounces) water chestnuts
 drained and sliced
1½ cups chicken broth
¼ cup soy sauce
2 tablespoons cornstarch
2 tablespoons dry white wine
¼ teaspoon powdered ginger

Pour oil into wok. Set heat control dial at 350° F. When light goes out, add garlic and scallions, and stir-fry 30 seconds. Push up sides of wok. Add green beans and stir-fry 2 minutes. Push up sides of wok. Add shrimp and stir-fry 2 minutes. Push up sides of wok. Add water chestnuts and stir-fry 1 minute. Push up sides of wok. Combine remaining ingredients and pour into wok. Simmer, stirring constantly until mixture thickens, about 1 minute. Stir in all ingredients from sides of wok. Heat until hot, about 1 minute.

Makes: 4 servings

Cauliflower with Crab Meat Sauce

Preparation time: 10 minutes
Cooking time: 15 minutes
Cooking technique: Steaming and Stir-frying

2 cups water
1 head (1½ pounds) cauliflower,
 cut into florets
2 tablespoons vegetable oil
1 can (7½ ounces) crab meat
3 scallions, chopped

1½ cups chicken broth
2 tablespoons dry white wine or
 dry sherry
1 tablespoon soy sauce
1 tablespoon cornstarch

Place steamer insert or rack in wok. Pour water into wok. Put cauliflower on insert. Cover. Set heat control dial at 250° F. Steam for 10 to 12 minutes or until cauliflower is tender. Remove cauliflower and steamer insert. Discard water. Wipe wok clean with paper towel. Pour oil into wok. Turn heat control dial to 350° F. When light goes out add crab meat and scallions. Stir-fry 1 minute. Remove and reserve. Combine remaining ingredients and pour mixture into wok. Simmer, stirring constantly until mixture thickens, about 1 minute. Return all ingredients to wok. Stir well to combine. Heat until hot, about 1 minute.

Makes: 4 servings

Sub Gum Pork Chow Mein

Preparation time: 20 minutes
Cooking time: 15 minutes
Cooking technique: Stir-frying

½ cup vegetable oil
1 pound boneless pork, cut in strips
1 large onion, cut in strips
2 cloves garlic, minced
1 can (6 ounces) water chestnuts,
  drained and sliced
½ pound snow peas
2 stalks celery, angle-sliced into
  ¼-inch slices
1 can (6½ ounces) bamboo shoots,
  drained

1 cup bean sprouts
¼ pound shrimp, cleaned,
  peeled and deveined
¼ pound boiled ham, cut in ½-inch
  strips
¼ pound mushrooms
2 cups chicken broth
½ cup soy sauce
3 tablespoons cornstarch
2 teaspoons brown sugar

Pour 2 tablespoons of oil into wok. Set heat control dial at 350° F. When light goes out stir-fry pork for 3 minutes, then push up sides of wok. Add onions and stir-fry 2 minutes. Push up sides of wok. Add garlic and stir-fry 30 seconds. Push up sides of wok. Add water chestnuts and snow peas and stir-fry for 2 minutes. Remove all stir-fried food from wok and reserve. Add 2 tablespoons oil and when light goes out add celery and stir-fry for 3 minutes. Push up sides of wok. Add bamboo shoots and bean sprouts and stir-fry 1 minute. Push up sides of wok. Add remaining oil. When light goes out add shrimp and ham. Stir-fry 1 minute and then push up sides of wok. Add mushrooms and stir-fry 30 seconds. Push up sides of wok. Combine remaining ingredients and pour mixture into wok, stirring constantly until mixture thickens, about 1 minute. Return all food to wok. Stir well. Heat about 2 minutes. Serve immediately.

Makes: 8 servings

Shrimp in Lobster Sauce

Preparation time: 30 minutes
Marinating time: 20 minutes
Cooking time: 10 minutes
Cooking technique: Stir-frying

MARINADE:

2 tablespoons soy sauce
2 tablespoons dry white wine
   or dry sherry
1½ cup chicken broth

½ teaspoon sugar
1 tablespoon cornstarch
¼ teaspoon fermented black beans,
   chopped

1 pound shrimp, cleaned,
   peeled and deveined
2 tablespoons vegetable oil
1 clove garlic

1 slice ginger root, cut ¼-inch thick
¼ pound ground pork
3 scallions, chopped
1 egg, well beaten

In a large bowl combine marinade ingredients. Add shrimp and marinate for 30 minutes. Pour oil into wok. Set heat control dial at 350° F. When light goes out add garlic and ginger root. Stir-fry 1 minute. Remove and discard. Add pork and stir-fry 3 minutes. Push up sides of wok. Remove shrimp from marinade. Add shrimp to wok and stir-fry 2 minutes. Push up sides of wok. Add scallions and stir-fry 1 minute. Pour marinade into wok. Stir constantly until mixture thickens, about 1 minute. Stir in all ingredients. Heat 1 minute or until hot. Turn heat control dial to "off." Stir in egg. Serve immediately.

Makes: 4 servings

Chicken *Chow Mein*

Preparation time: 20 minutes
Cooking time: 15 minutes
Cooking technique: Stir-frying

⅓ cup vegetable oil
1 slice ginger root, ¼-inch thick
1 clove garlic, crushed
2 whole chicken breasts, skinned,
    boned and cut in thin strips
4 stalks celery, angle-cut ⅛-inch
    thick
1 can (8½ ounces) water chestnuts,
    drained and sliced
3 cups chopped Chinese cabbage

1 can (8½ ounces) sliced bamboo
    shoots drained
6 scallions, sliced
1½ cups chicken broth
½ cup soy sauce
2 teaspoons brown sugar
2 tablespoons cornstarch
2 tablespoons white wine
2 cups cooked egg noodles

Pour 2 tablespoons oil into wok. Set heat control dial at 350° F. When light goes out add ginger root and garlic and stir-fry 1 minute. Remove and discard. Add chicken. Stir-fry 2 minutes. Remove and reserve. Add more oil as needed. When light goes out add celery and water chestnuts. Stir-fry 2 minutes. Remove and reserve. Add Chinese cabbage, bamboo shoots and scallions. Stir-fry 1 minute. Remove and reserve. Combine remaining ingredients and pour mixture into wok. Simmer, stirring constantly until mixture thickens, about 1 minute. Return all ingredients to wok. Stir well to combine. Heat 1 minute. Serve over egg noodles.

Makes: 6 to 8 servings

Butterfly Shrimp and Bacon

Preparation time: 30 minutes
Marinating time: 20 minutes
Cooking time: 20 minutes
Cooking technique: Deep-frying, Stir-frying

MARINADE:

¼ cup soy sauce
¼ cup chicken broth
2 tablespoons white wine

½ teaspoon cornstarch
1 teaspoon sugar

1 pound large shrimp, cleaned,
    shelled, deveined
3 cups oil

BATTER:

1 egg, well beaten
1 cup all-purpose flour
1 teaspoon salt

¼ teaspoon pepper
¾ cup milk

4 slices bacon, cut into ½-inch
    pieces

3 scallions, minced
1 clove garlic, minced

In a large bowl, combine marinade ingredients. Marinate shrimp for 20 minutes. Set heat control dial at 425° F. Pour oil into wok. While oil is heating combine batter ingredients. Remove shrimp from marinade; reserve marinade. Dip shrimp into batter. When light goes out deep-fry about ⅓ of the shrimp for 3 to 5 minutes or until deep golden brown. Remove and drain on tempura rack or absorbent paper towels. Continue frying shrimp until all are cooked. Carefully drain oil from wok. Turn heat control dial to 350° F. Add bacon and fry until crisp, about 3 minutes. Push up sides of wok. Add scallions and garlic and stir-fry 1 minute. Carefully remove bacon fat. Pour reserved marinade into wok. Stir in bacon and scallions. Heat, stirring constantly until mixture thickens, about 1 minute. Pour over shrimp and toss well to coat. Serve immediately.

Makes: 4 servings

Steamed Stuffed Mushrooms

Preparation time: 20 minutes
Cooking time: 10 minutes
Cooking techniques: Stir-frying, Steaming

⅓ cup vegetable oil
½ pound ground pork
2 cloves garlic, minced
3 scallions, minced
1 teaspoon sesame seeds
1 pound mushrooms, stems
  removed and chopped

½ cup chicken broth
1 tablespoon soy sauce
2 teaspoons dry white wine or
  dry sherry
2 teaspoons cornstarch
½ teaspoon salt
¼ teaspoon pepper
2 cups water

Pour oil into wok. Set heat control dial at 350° F. When light goes out add pork and stir-fry until lightly browned, about 2 minutes. Push up sides of wok. Add garlic, scallions, sesame seeds, mushroom stems and stir-fry 1 minute. Stir in pork. Combine remaining ingredients except water and mushroom caps and pour into wok. Stir well to combine and simmer 1 minute. Turn heat control to "off." Remove mixture and clean wok. Fill mushroom caps with pork mixture. Pour water into wok. Place steamer insert or rack into wok. Place mushrooms on rack. Cover. Set heat control dial at 250° F. and steam for 5 minutes. Serves as hors d'oeuvres.

Makes: about 24

Sweet and Sour Chicken

Preparation time: 20 minutes
Cooking time: 10 minutes
Cooking technique: Stir-frying

2 tablespoons vegetable oil
½ cup slivered almonds
1 medium onion, chopped
3 green peppers, cut in 1-inch
  pieces
2 boneless chicken breasts,
  skinned and cut into bite-size
  pieces

1 can (1 pound 4 ounces) pineapple
  chunks, undrained
2 tablespoons soy sauce
¼ cup vinegar
½ teaspoon ground ginger
2 tablespoons cornstarch

Pour oil into wok, set heat control dial at 350° F. When light goes out, add almonds and stir-fry 30 seconds. Push up sides of wok. Add onions and green peppers and stir-fry 2 minutes. Push up sides of wok. Add chicken. Stir-fry 2 minutes. Push up sides of wok. Add pineapple chunks, reserving liquid. Stir-fry 1 minute. Push up sides of wok. Combine pineapple juice with remaining ingredients and pour mixture into wok. Simmer, stirring constantly until mixture thickens, about 1 minute. Stir in all ingredients from sides of wok. Heat 1 minute. Serve with rice.

Makes: 4 servings

Chicken-filled Fried Dumplings

Preparation time: 30 minutes
Cooking time: 5 minutes
Cooking technique: Deep-frying

2 cups flour
⅔ cup boiling water
¼ cup cold water

FILLING:

¼ pound boneless chicken	**1 tablespoon Sweet and Sour Sauce**
2 ounces boneless pork	**1 egg**
1 clove garlic	**2 teaspoons cornstarch**
3 mushrooms	**1 teaspoon sesame seeds**
2 scallions	**1 teaspoon salt**
½ teaspoon hoisin sauce	**¼ teaspoon pepper**

2 cups vegetable oil

In a large bowl combine flour and hot and cold water. With lightly floured hands knead well to form a soft ball. Cover. Allow to stand for 15 minutes. While dough is standing place all filling ingredients into food processor or blender and puree. Pour oil into wok. Set heat control dial at 425° F. While oil is heating roll out dough as thin as possible on lightly floured board. Cut into 24 three-inch circles with a biscuit cutter or the top of a glass. Spoon about 1 teaspoon of filling into the center of half of the dough rounds. Place a second round of dough on top of each filled round and crimp edges all around with a fork, making 12 dumplings. When light goes out carefully add dumplings to oil. Deep-fry until well browned, about 2 minutes per side. Drain on tempura rack or absorbent paper towels. Serve as an hors d'oeuvre with Sweet and Sour Sauce (page 23), Plum Sauce (page 22), and Mustard Sauce (page 23).

Makes: 12 dumplings

Japan

Japan, the "Land of the Rising Sun," is a mountainous and hilly island nation where there is very little flat land for farming. This does not stop the farmers from producing abundant crops but there are simply too many people to live off the land and food is not always plentiful. It becomes necessary to obtain food and other raw materials from other countries.

Japan is made up of four large and many small islands. There are many problems brought about by nature. Tidal waves, typhoons and earthquakes are not uncommon. Each causes great damage, particularly in coastal areas.

The climate varies from tropical to extremely cold. Rain is plentiful in the South, especially in the summer when it is most needed for the growing crops.

Rice is the major crop but soybeans,

mulberries, wheat and barley are also grown in quantity.

Rice farming and fishing are important means of livelihood for many Japanese. Rice is the main food and is served at almost every meal. Bean curd and fish are also important staples of the diet.

Many people are a little skeptical about trying Japanese food because it is well known that many dishes include raw fish. However, if you are willing to try it you may be pleasantly surprised at how tasty some of these "raw" fish dishes are. In fact, they are cooked by marinating. For those not quite so adventuresome, there are many delicious foods which are prepared in the Japanese manner and are included here for your enjoyment.

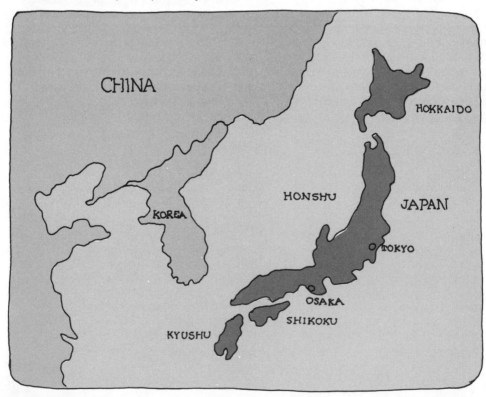

Steamed Egg Custard

Preparation time: 5 minutes
Cooking time: 30 minutes
Cooking technique: Steaming

6 eggs
½ teaspoon salt
¼ teaspoon pepper
2 tablespoon dry white wine or
  dry sherry
1 cup chicken broth

4 mushrooms, finely chopped
2 scallions, finely chopped
1 teaspoon soy sauce
1 can (6 ounces) crab meat,
  drained
4 cups water

In a large mixing bowl combine all ingredients except water. Pour mixture into a buttered 8-inch round cake pan. Pour water into wok. Place steamer insert or rack in wok. Put pan on rack and place a piece of wax paper over dish. Cover wok. Set heat control dial at 250° F. Steam until a knife inserted 1-inch from center comes out clean, about 30 to 35 minutes.

Makes: 6 servings

Clam Fritters

Preparation time: 10 minutes
Cooking time: 5 minutes
Cooking technique: Deep-frying

3 cups vegetable oil
2 tablespoons chopped almonds
¼ cup all-purpose flour
2 eggs
1 can (6½ ounces) minced clams,
  drained

2 tablespoons dried coconut
⅛ teaspoon pepper
¼ teaspoon salt
2 scallions, chopped

Pour oil into wok. Set heat control dial at 425° F. In a small bowl combine all ingredients. When light goes out drop batter by heaping teaspoonfuls into hot oil. Deep-fry until golden brown, about 3 minutes. Drain on tempura rack or absorbent paper towels.

Makes: 12 to 15 fritters

Japanese Cabbage Rolls

Preparation time: 20 minutes
Cooking time: 30 minutes
Cooking technique: Simmering

1 cup water
24 Chinese cabbage leaves
   (about 2 pounds)
2 cups beef broth
1 tablespoon sake or dry white wine
½ pound ground pork
¼ pound ground beef

1 small carrot, finely grated
½ small onion, finely chopped
1 clove garlic, minced
2 teaspoons soy sauce
1 teaspoon cornstarch
1 teaspoon salt
¼ teaspoon powdered ginger

Pour water into wok. Set heat control dial at 250° F. When water begins to boil add cabbage. Boil for 10 minutes. Remove and dry on paper towels. Discard water. Pour beef broth and sake into wok. While liquid is coming to a boil combine remaining ingredients. Spoon about 2 tablespoons of meat mixture into cabbage leaves. Fold sides into each other and roll up jelly roll style. Tie with thread. When broth begins to boil add cabbage rolls. Cover. Simmer for 15 to 20 minutes.

Makes: 24

Japanese Chicken and Vegetables

Preparation time: 15 minutes
Marinating time: 1 hour
Cooking time: 10 minutes
Cooking technique: Stir-frying

MARINADE:
1 cup chicken broth
¼ cup soy sauce

2 teaspoons white vinegar
1 teaspoon sugar

2 chicken breasts, skinned, boned,
   and cut into 1-inch chunks
¼ cup vegetable oil
3 stalks celery, angle-cut into thin
   slices

3 scallions, sliced
2 cloves garlic, minced
6 mushrooms, sliced
4 eggs, well beaten

In a large bowl combine marinade ingredients. Marinate chicken 1 hour. Remove chicken from marinade and reserve marinade. Pour 2 tablespoons oil into wok. Set heat control dial at 350° F. When light goes out add celery and stir-fry for 2 minutes. Push up sides of wok. Add scallions and garlic and stir-fry 1 minute. Push up sides of wok. Add remaining oil and when light goes out add chicken and stir-fry 3 minutes. Push up sides of wok. Add mushrooms and stir-fry 1 minute. Push up sides of wok. Pour marinade into wok. Simmer, stirring constantly, until mixture thickens, about 1 minute. Stir in all ingredients. Add eggs and stir well. Cook 2 minutes. Serve immediately over rice.

Makes: 6 servings

Deep-fried Sweet and Sour Fish Filets

Preparation time: 10 minutes
Cooking time: 10 minutes
Cooking technique: Deep-frying, Stir-frying

3 cups vegetable oil
1 egg
⅓ cup all-purpse flour
1 teaspoon salt
¼ teaspoon pepper
1 pound fish filets
2 scallions, chopped
1 clove garlic, crushed

1 can (6 ounces) water chestnuts,
   drained and sliced
2 tablespoons soy sauce
2 teaspoons cornstarch
1 can (1 pound) pineapple chunks,
   with liquid
2 tablespoons white vinegar

Pour oil into wok. Set heat control dial at 425° F. While oil is heating combine egg, flour, salt and pepper in a bowl to form a batter. Dip fish filets into batter. When light goes out carefully add fish and deep-fry until golden brown, about 5 minutes. Remove and drain on tempura rack or absorbent paper towels. Carefully remove all but 1 tablespoon of oil from wok. Add scallions, garlic and water chestnuts and stir-fry 1 minute. Push up sides of wok. Combine remaining ingredients. Pour mixture into wok and simmer, stirring constantly until mixture thickens, about 1 minute. Stir in vegetables. Heat until hot, about 1 minute. Pour over fish and serve immediately.

Makes: 4 servings

Kung Bow Chicken

Preparation time: 50 minutes
Cooking time: 10 minutes
Cooking technique: Stir-frying

8 dried black mushrooms
2 tablespoons vegetable oil
1 clove garlic, mashed
2 tablespoons salted peanuts,
   coarsely chopped
2 stalks celery, angle-cut
   ¼-inch thick
1 large chicken breast, skinned,
   boned and cut into bite sized
   pieces

1 can (8 ounces) sliced bamboo
   shoots, drained
3 tablespoons soy sauce
¼ teaspoon crushed red pepper
2 tablespoons dry white wine
   or dry sherry
1 teaspoon cornstarch

Soak mushrooms in a small amount of water until soft, about 45 minutes. Drain and reserve. Pour oil into wok. Set heat control dial at 350° F. When light goes out add garlic and stir-fry 1 minute. Remove and discard. Add peanuts and stir-fry 20 seconds. Push up sides of wok. Add celery and stir-fry 2 minutes. Push up sides of wok. Add chicken and stir-fry 3 minutes. Push up sides of wok. Add bamboo shoots and reserved mushrooms. Stir-fry 1 minute and push up sides of wok. Combine remaining ingredients and pour mixture into wok. Simmer, stirring constantly until mixture thickens, about 1 minute. Stir in all ingredients from sides of wok and heat until hot, about 1 minute.

Makes: 4 servings

Japanese Fried Fish Steaks

Preparation time: 5 minutes
Cooking time: 5 minutes
Cooking technique: Shallow-frying

⅓ cup vegetable oil
1 clove garlic, mashed
1 slice ginger root, cut
  ½-inch thick
4 cod or salmon steaks (about 1¼ to
  1½ pounds) cut ½-inch thick
1 teaspoon salt
¼ teaspoon pepper

1¼ cups chicken broth
2 tablespoons lemon juice
2 tablespoons soy sauce
2 tablespoons sake or
  dry white wine
1 tablespoon cornstarch
1 teaspoon sugar

Pour oil into wok. Set heat control dial at 350° F. When light goes out add garlic and ginger. Stir-fry 1 minute. Remove and discard. Add fish and shallow- fry until lightly browned, about 5 minutes on each side. Remove fish to a platter and cover with aluminum foil. Carefully discard oil. Combine remaining ingredients and pour into wok. Simmer, stirring constantly until mixture thickens, about 1 minute. Pour over fish and serve immediately.

Makes: 4 servings

Pork Cutlets *Teriyaki*

Preparation time: 10 minutes
Marinating time: 1 hour
Cooking time: 20 minutes
Cooking technique: Shallow-frying, Simmering

MARINADE:
¼ cup soy sauce
1 tablespoon cornstarch
2 tablespoons white wine
1 cup chicken broth

2 scallions, finely minced
1 clove garlic, minced
⅛ teaspoon powdered ginger
1 tablespoon brown sugar

1½ pounds lean boneless pork loin
  cut in ½-inch slices
¼ cup vegetable oil

In a large bowl combine all marinade ingredients. Add pork and marinate for 1 hour. Pour oil into wok. Set heat control dial at 350° F. Pat cutlets dry with paper towel. When light goes out fry pork until well browned, about 5 minutes per side. Remove and reserve. Discard oil. Wipe wok clean with a paper towel. Pour marinade into wok, stirring constantly until mixture thickens, about 1 minute. Return pork to wok. Turn heat control dial to 250° F. and simmer for 5 minutes. Serve with rice.

Makes: 6 servings

Chicken *Sukiyaki*

Preparation time: 10 minutes
Cooking time: 10 minutes
Cooking technique: Stir-frying

⅓ cup vegetable oil
1 large onion, cut in strips
1 can (6 ounces) water chestnuts,
    drained and sliced
1 cup bean sprouts
2 whole chicken breasts, skinned,
    boned and cut in strips

¾ pound bok choy cut in 1-inch slices
¼ pound mushrooms, sliced
2 cups chicken broth
½ cup soy sauce
2 teaspoons brown sugar

Pour 2 tablespoons oil into wok. Set heat control dial at 350° F. When light goes out add onions and stir-fry 2 minutes. Push up sides of wok. Add water chestnuts and stir-fry 1 minute. Push up sides of wok. Add 2 tablespoons oil and when light goes out add bean sprouts and stir-fry 30 seconds. Remove and reserve all ingredients. Add chicken and stir-fry 3 minutes. Push up sides of wok. Add remaining oil. When light goes out add bok choy and stir-fry 2 minutes. Push up sides of wok. Add mush rooms and stir-fry for 30 seconds. Push up sides of wok. Combine reamaining in-gredients. Pour mixture into wok. Return all ingredients to wok. Stir well to combine. Heat until hot, about 2 minutes. Serve immediately.

Makes: 8 servings

Tempura

Preparation time: 15 minutes
Cooking time: 15 minutes
Cooking technique: Deep-frying

3 cups vegetable oil
¾ pound fish steak, cut
  in ½-inch cubes
¾ pound shrimp, cleaned,
  shelled and deveined
1 zucchini, cut in ½-inch slices

½ pound cauliflower, broken
  into small florets
¼ pound bok choy, cut
  in ½-inch slices
¼ pound mushrooms
1 small onion, cut in strips

BATTER:
1 cup cornstarch
4 egg whites
½ cup water

1 teaspoon salt
¼ teaspoon pepper

Pour oil into wok. Set heat control dial at 425° F. While oil is heating cut and prepare ingredients. Combine batter ingredients in a large bowl. Coat all ingredients with batter. When light goes out place a few of each item in wok and deep-fry fish for 3 minutes, shrimp, zucchini, cauliflower and bok choy for 2 minutes, mushrooms and onions 1 minute. Drain on tempura rack or absorbent paper towels. Tempura may be prepared at the dinner table by your guests. Each person should be given a dish of dipping sauces and a long handled fondue fork. Dipping sauces include Mustard Sauce on page 23, Plum Sauce on page 22 and Sweet and Sour Sauce on page 23.

Makes: 8 servings

Japanese Deep-fried Fish Cakes

Preparation time: 5 minutes
Cooking time: 10 minutes
Cooking technique: Deep-frying

3 cups vegetable oil
1 pound flounder or cod filets
6 water chestnuts
2 scallions
1 tablespoon cornstarch

3 mushrooms
1 teaspoon soy sauce
1 teaspoon salt
¼ teaspoon pepper
3 tablespoons cornstarch

Pour oil into wok. Set heat control dial at 425° F. Place all ingredients except the last 3 tablespoons cornstarch in food processor or blender and grind. Form mixture into 8 fishcakes and roll in cornstarch. When light goes out carefully place fish cakes in hot oil. Deep-fry until golden brown, about 5 minutes. Drain on tempura rack or absorbent paper towels.

Makes: 8 cakes

Fish Steaks with Spinach Puree

Preparation time: 5 minutes
Cooking time: 10 minutes
Cooking technique: Steaming

2 tablespoons soy sauce
1 teaspoon sake or dry white wine
1 pound cod or halibut fish
  steaks cut 1-inch thick
2 cups water
½ pound spinach, cleaned

3 eggs, well beaten
1 tablespoon sugar
1 tablespoon vinegar
¼ teaspoon pepper
1 teaspoon vegetable oil

Combine soy sauce and sake. Brush both sides of fish with the mixture. Place steamer insert or rack into wok. Pour water into wok. Set heat control dial at 250° F. Place fish on one half of the insert and the spinach on the other. Cover wok and steam for 8 minutes. Remove fish to a platter and cover with aluminum foil. Remove insert and discard water. Wipe wok clean with a paper towel. Place spinach and remaining ingredients except oil in food processor or blender and puree. Pour oil into wok. Set heat control dial at 225° F. Add mixture. Simmer, stirring constantly until mixture thickens, about 1 minute. Spoon mixture over fish and serve immediately.

Makes: 4 servings

Beef *Sukiyaki*

Preparation time: 25 minutes
Cooking time: 15 minutes
Cooking technique: Stir-frying

1½ pounds sirloin steak,
   very thinly sliced
6 scallions, thinly sliced
¼ pound mushrooms, sliced
1 can water chestnuts (8 ounces),
   drained and sliced

1 package (3¾ ounces) cellophane
   noodles, pre-soaked, drained, and
   cut into 4-inch lengths
½ pound fresh spinach, stems
   removed
½ pound soy bean cake (*tofu*), cut in
   1-inch cubes

SAUCE:
½ cup soy sauce
1 cup beef broth
⅓ cup vegetable oil

2 tablespoons saki or dry white wine
2 tablespoons sugar

Arrange meat down the center of a 12-inch round or oblong platter. Place prepared vegetables in rows along either side of meat. Cover with plastic wrap and refrigerate until you are ready to cook at the table.

To prepare sauce, combine soy sauce, beef broth, wine and sugar in a small pitcher.

To cook, pour 2 tablespoons oil into wok. Set heat control dial at 350° F. When light goes out, add onions and stir-fry 1 minute. Push up sides of wok. Add mushrooms, and stir-fry 1 minute. Push up sides of wok. Add 2 tablespoons oil, and when light goes out add water chestnuts. Stir-fry 1 minute. Remove and reserve all ingredients. Add 2 tablespoons oil. Add one-third of the meat and stir-fry 2 minutes. Push up sides of wok. Add one-third more meat and stir-fry 2 minutes. Push up sides of wok. Add remaining oil and when light goes out add remaining meat. Stir-fry 2 minutes Push up sides of wok. Add sauce ingredients. Return all stir-fry items. Add cellophane noodles and stir well to combine. Place spinach and bean curd on top of the ingredients. Cover and steam for about 2 minutes or until spinach is limp. Serve in small bowls with bowls of hot rice.

Makes: 6 to 8 servings

Beef *Teriyaki*

Preparation time: 10 minutes
Marinating time: 1 hour
Cooking time: 2 to 3 minutes
Cooking technique: Stir-fry

MARINADE:

1 teaspoon ground ginger
½ cup soy sauce
2 tablespoons honey
¼ cup pineapple juice

2 tablespoons chopped parsley
1 clove garlic, minced
1 tablespoon chopped onion
1 tablespoon cornstarch
½ cup water

1 pound beef sirloin tip, cut into thin
  2-inch strips
2 tablespoons cooking oil

In a shallow baking dish combine marinade ingredients. Add meat and marinate 1 hour. Remove meat from marinade and reserve marinade.

Pour oil into wok. Set heat control dial at 350° F. When light goes out, add half of the meat and stir-fry 2 minutes. Push up sides of wok. Add remaining meat and stir-fry 2 minutes. Push up sides of wok. Pour marinade into wok, stirring constantly until mixture thickens, about 30 seconds. Stir in meat from sides of the wok and serve immediately.

Makes: 4 servings

Korea

Korea is a very mountainous country and much of the land is unsuitable for cultivation. Most of the flat useable land is in South Korea and therefore that area is very densely populated. South Koreans are almost totally dependent on the land for their livelihood. Many are farmers and a good many of the rest work at processing the food.

The climate in the South lends itself to agriculture. The summers are hot and moist and the winters are mild. In the North the winters are longer and more severe.

Rice is the main crop of the South but barley is also grown there in the lowlands. The hilly land is good for the production of millet, wheat, soybeans and corn. Fruits such as apples, pears, mandarin oranges, plums and mulberries also thrive in this hilly terrain.

Fishing is an important source of income for the people of the coastal areas. The fish are abundant and are therefore an important part of the diet. The cooking of Korea is more complex than that of Japan but nowhere near as sophisticated as that of China. Korean food is quite spicy because of the liberal use of dried, crushed red peppers and garlic. The main staples of the diet are rice, beans, fish, bean sprouts and sesame seeds.

There are some interesting and flavorful recipes in this section. Many are spicy but none are overpowering.

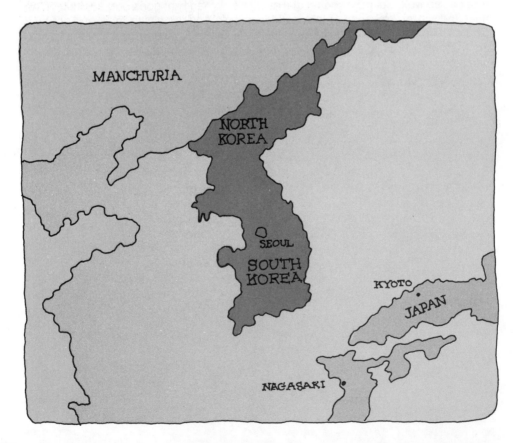

Korean Fried Steak

Preparation time: 5 minutes
Marinating time: 3 hours
Cooking time: 10 minutes
Cooking technique: Pan-frying

MARINADE:

4 scallions, chopped
¼ cup soy sauce
1 tablespoon sesame oil
1 tablespoon brown sugar

1 clove garlic
½ cup water
1 tablespoon cornstarch

1 flank steak (1 pound) angle-cut
   into thin slices
¼ cup vegetable oil

In a large bowl combine marinade ingredients. Place steak in bowl. Cover and marinate for 3 hours. Pour 2 tablespoons oil into wok. Set heat control dial at 350° F. When light goes out add steak, 5 or 6 pieces at a time. Reserve marinade. Fry 1 to 2 minutes per side, depending on desired doneness. Remove and reserve. Continue to fry steak until all steak is cooked. Add oil as needed. When all steak is fried pour reserved marinade into wok. Simmer, stirring constantly until mixture thickens, about 1 minute. Return meat to wok and stir to combine. Heat until hot, about 1 minute.

Makes: 4 to 6 servings

Korean Vegetable Fritters

Preparation time: 10 minutes
Cooking time: 10 minutes
Cooking technique: Deep-frying

3 cups vegetable oil
1 carrot, cut in 1-inch pieces
1 large potato, cut in 1-inch
   pieces, boiled and drained
¼ cup cooked rice
1 small onion, cut in quarters

1 clove garlic
1 tablespoon flour
1 teaspoon salt
¼ teaspoon pepper
1 egg
2 slices bread

Pour oil into wok. Set heat control dial at 425° F. Combine all other ingredients and place in food processor or blender. Puree. When light goes out, drop batter by heaping teaspoonfuls into hot oil. Deep-fry until golden brown, about 3 to 5 minutes. Drain on tempura rack or absorbent paper towels.

Makes: about 2 dozen

Korean Meatball Noodle Soup

Preparation time: 45 minutes
Cooking time: 1 hour
Cooking technique: Simmering

MEATBALLS:

1 pound ground beef
1 medium onion, minced
1 teaspoon salt
¼ teaspoon pepper
½ cup vegetable oil

2 teaspoons sesame seeds
½ cup bread crumbs
1 egg

SOUP:

3 scallions, chopped
1 clove garlic, minced
1 can (20 ounces) crushed
   tomatoes

¼ to ½ teaspoon crushed
   red pepper
6 cups beef broth
2 cups fine egg noodles

In a large bowl combine all meatball ingredients. Form mixture into 60 (½-inch) meatballs. Pour oil into wok. Set heat control dial at 350° F. When light goes out shallow-fry ⅓ of the meatballs until well browned on all sides, about 3 minutes. Repeat until all meatballs are cooked. While meatballs are frying prepare soup ingredients. Remove meatballs and reserve. Discard oil. Wipe wok clean with paper towel. Add remaining ingredients except egg noodles to wok. Return meatballs. Cover. Turn heat control to 250° F. Simmer for 40 minutes. Add egg noodles. Stir well. Cover. Simmer until noodles are tender, about 10 minutes.

Makes: 8 servings

Korean Stuffed Eggplant

Preparation time: 10 minutes
Cooking time: 25 minutes
Cooking technique: Steaming

2 small eggplants (¾ pound each)
   unpeeled and cut in half lengthwise
1 medium onion, finely chopped
2 cloves garlic, minced
1 tablespoon sesame seeds
½ pound ground beef
¼ pound ground pork

6 mushrooms, chopped
1 cup beef broth
1 tablespoon soy sauce
1 teaspoon salt
¼ teaspoon pepper
2 cups water

Scoop out inside pulp of eggplant, Cut pulp into ¼-inch cubes. Combine eggplant with remaining ingredients. Fill eggplant shells with mixture. Pour water into wok. Place steamer insert into wok. Place filled eggplant halves on insert. Cover. Steam for 25 minutes. Sprinkle with paprika and serve.

Makes: 4 servings

Korean Chicken Stew

Preparation time: 10 minutes
Marinating time: 30 minutes
Cooking time: 40 minutes
Cooking technique: Stewing

MARINADE:

1½ cups chicken broth
¼ cup soy sauce
1 tablespoon sesame seeds
1 teaspoon brown sugar

½ teaspoon pepper
1 small onion, chopped
2 cloves garlic, minced

1 chicken (2½ to 3 pounds),
   cut in pieces
12 small white onions, peeled
3 carrots, cleaned, cut in 1-inch
   pieces

¼ pound mushrooms, sliced
1 can (6½ ounces) sliced bamboo
   shoots, drained

Pour all marinade ingredients into wok, stir well to combine. Add chicken and marinate 30 minutes. Cover. Set heat control dial at 250° F. Simmer for 20 minutes. Serve with noodles.

Makes: 4 to 6 servings

Korean Rice and Beans

Preparation time: 5 minutes
Cooking time: 1 hour 55 minutes
Cooking technique: Sautéeing, Simmering

2 tablespoons vegetable oil
1 onion, finely chopped
1 clove garlic, minced
1 teaspoon salt
½ to 1 teaspoon crushed red pepper

2½ cups beef broth
1½ cups water
½ pound dried red kidney beans
⅓ cup raw rice

Pour oil into wok. Set heat control at 350° F. When light goes out add onions and sauté for 2 minutes. Add garlic and sauté 30 seconds. Add salt, pepper, broth, water and kidney beans. Cover. Turn heat control dial to 250° F. and simmer for 1 hour 30 minutes, stirring occasionally. Add rice and stir well. Cover. Simmer 20 minutes.

Makes: 4 servings

Korean Cinnamon Cakes

Preparation time: 5 minutes
Cooking time: 5 minutes
Cooking technique: Deep-frying

2 cups vegetable oil
1 cup all-purpose flour
½ teaspoon salt
1 teaspoon baking powder
2 teaspoons sugar

¾ cup water
2 tablespoons sesame seeds
1 teaspoon cinnamon
1 tablespoon sugar

Pour oil into wok. Set heat control dial at 425° F. In a small bowl, combine flour, salt, baking powder and sugar. Stir in water to form a batter. When light goes out spoon batter by the tablespoonful into hot oil. Fry until golden brown on both sides, about 5 minutes. Combine remaining ingredients. Drain cakes on tempura rack or absorbent paper towels. Roll in sugar mixture while still hot.

Makes: About 18

Hawaii

Hawaii is a group of eight major islands in the South Pacific. The climate is semi-tropical. The cool north-east trade wind and the ocean help keep the temperature somewhat constant. It rarely gets colder than 65° F. or warmer than 75° F. It is a lush tropical paradise where trees, shrubs and plants bloom everywhere.

Before its discovery by Captain James Cook in 1778, Hawaiians lived entirely from the fruits of the land and sea. They ate yams, taro root, coconut, pork, chicken and an endless variety of fish and seaweed found off the islands. When the missionaries arrived in l820, along with Christianity they brought many new foods.

In 1852 the oriental immigration and influence began. The first immigrants came from Canton in the south of China. They brought with them not only their culture and religion but the staples of their diet; rice, soybeans and a large variety of sauces

In 1868 Japanese from Hiroshima and Okinawa emigrated to Hawaii. They brought their diet staples of rice and a variety of bean products. Their cultural influence has been great on the islands and included the introduction of Buddhism to the natives.

The next oriental immigrants were from Korea and they also made a major contribution to what is now known as Hawaiian cuisine. The use of red peppers, garlic, sesame oil and sesame seeds can be traced directly to the Koreans.

The last Pacific influence was from the Phillipines. Many of the fruits and vegetables that are native to the Phillipines were also found in Hawaii but the Filipino methods of cooking were different. Filipino cuisine had been influenced by the Chinese and Spanish and this Eurasian influence found its way into Hawaiian cookery.

The only strictly European influence to the Hawaiian style of cooking was Portugese. These immigrants introduced spicy sausages, sweet breads and delicious holiday pastries.

In time all these cultures and cuisines blended into one — Hawaiian. The recipes in this chapter show the various European and Oriental influences. Here is a delightful blend of many cultures to be tried and savored.

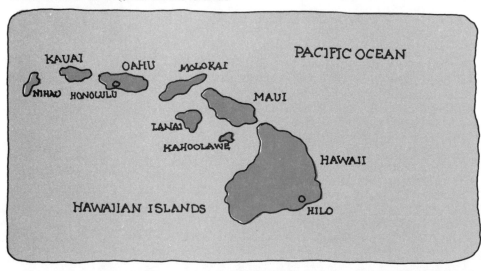

93

Hawaiian Spareribs

Preparation time: 10 minutes
Marinating time: 1 hour
Cooking time: 20 minutes
Cooking technique: Shallow-frying, Stir-frying

1 rack (2½ to 3 pounds) pork
  spareribs
	1 can (20 ounces) pineapple chunks
	  with liquid

MARINADE:

2 tablespoons soy sauce 1 slice ginger root, cut ¼-inch thick	1 clove garlic, crushed ¼ cup white vinegar 1 tablespoon brown sugar

¼ cup vegetable oil
1 medium onion, cut in strips
1 medium green pepper,
  cut in strips
	12 marachino cherries,
	  without stems

Cut pork rack into individual ribs. In a large bowl combine soy sauce, ginger root, garlic, white vinegar, brown sugar and liquid from pineapple. Place ribs into bowl and marinate for 1 hour. While the ribs are marinating, prepare remaining ingredients. Pour oil into wok. Set heat control dial at 350° F. While oil is heating remove ribs from marinade and pat dry with paper towels. Reserve marinade. When light goes out add ribs to wok and shallow-fry until ribs are well browned, about 6 minutes per side. Remove and reserve. Add onions and peppers and stir-fry for 2 minutes. Remove and reserve. Discard oil. Wipe out wok with paper towels. Pour reserved marinade into wok. Simmer, stirring constantly until mixture thickens, about 1 minute. Return ribs, onions, peppers, pineapple chunks and cherries to wok. Stir well to combine. Heat until hot, about 1 minute. Serve immediately.

Makes: 4 to 6 servings

Island Fried Fish

Preparation time: 10 minutes
Marinating time: 30 minutes
Cooking time: 5 minutes
Cooking technique: Deep-frying

2 pounds fish fillets, fresh or frozen,
    thawed

MARINADE:
¼ cup soy sauce
2 tablespoons lemon juice
½ teaspoon sugar

3 cups vegetable oil
½ cup cornstarch
½ cup all-purpose flour
1 tablespoon baking powder
1 teaspoon salt

¼ teaspoon pepper
½ cup water
1 egg, beaten
Pineapple Sauce

In a large bowl, combine marinade ingredients. Add fish and marinate 10 minutes.

Pour oil into wok. Set heat control dial at 425°F. In a large bowl combine dry ingredients. Combine water and egg and blend into flour mixture. Dip fish into batter. When light goes out place 3 or 4 pieces into wok and fry until golden brown, about 5 to 6 minutes. Drain on tempura rack or absorbent paper towels. Keep warm, and continue to fry until all fish is fried. Pour Pineapple Sauce over fish and serve.

Makes: 6 servings

Pineapple Sauce

Preparation time: 2 minutes
Cooking time: 3 minutes
Cooking technique: Simmering

1 can (1 pound 4½ ounces)
    crushed pineapple, undrained

2 tablespoons cornstarch
¼ cup cold water

Place pineapple in wok. Set heat control dial at 250° F. Dissolve cornstarch in water. Add gradually to pineapple and cook until thickened, stirring constantly. Serve over Island Fried Fish.

Makes: 2 cups

Hawaiian Pork Chops and Pineapple

Preparation time: 10 minutes
Cooking time: 25 minutes
Cooking technique: Shallow-frying, Simmering

2 slices bread
¼ cup slivered almonds
6 pork chops, cut ½-inch thick
¼ cup all-purpose flour
1 egg, beaten
¼ cup milk
½ cup vegetable oil

1 can (20 ounces) crushed pineapple,
  with liquid
2½ cups chicken broth
2 tablespoons brown sugar
2 tablespoons cornstarch
1 tablespoon soy sauce
2 tablespoons white wine
½ teaspoon allspice

Place bread and almonds in food processor or blender and grind. Remove and reserve. Dredge pork chops in flour. Combine egg and milk and dip floured chops in mixture. Dredge chops in reserved bread crumb mixture. Pour oil into wok and set heat control dial at 350° F. When light goes out add pork chops 3 at a time and shallow-fry until well browned, about 5 to 8 minutes per side. While chops are cooking, combine remaining ingredients. When all chops are browned remove and reserve. Discard oil. Wipe wok clean with a paper towel. Add combined remaining ingredients to wok. Return chops. Turn heat control dial to 250° F. Cover and simmmer for 8 minutes. Garnish with pineapple slices if desired, and serve with buttered rice or noodles.

Makes: 4 to 6 servings

Pickled Fish

Preparation time: 5 minutes
Cooking time: 10 minutes
Marinating time: 3 hours
Cooking technique: Shallow-frying

½ cup vegetable oil
¾ cup all-purpose flour
1 teaspoon salt
¼ teaspoon pepper

½ teaspoon paprika
½ teaspoon curry
1 pound flounder or sole filets,
   cut in 2-inch pieces

MARINADE:
¾ cup white vinegar
2 tablespoons brown sugar
¾ cup water

6 mint leaves (optional)
1 large onion, sliced

Pour oil into wok. Set heat control dial at 350° F. While oil is heating combine flour, salt, pepper, paprika and curry. Dredge fish in flour mixture, shaking off excess. When oil is hot shallow-fry fish until lightly browned, about 5 minutes. In a 13 x 9 x 4-inch oblong dish combine marinade ingredients. Place fried fish into marinade being sure that all the fish is covered. Marinate for about 3 hours before serving. Serve cold as first course or hors d'oeuvre.

Makes: 6 servings

Hawaiian Deep-fried Crab Cakes

Preparation time: 5 minutes
Cooking time: 5 minutes
Cooking technique: Deep-frying

3 cups vegetable oil
¼ cup slivered almonds
3 slices bread
1 medium onion
1 clove garlic, minced
1 teaspoon salt

¼ teaspoon pepper
¼ cup coconut
2 cans (6½ ounces each)
   crab meat
1 egg

Pour oil into wok. Set heat control dial at 425° F. Place almonds and bread in food processor or blender and grind. Remove and reserve. Combine remaining ingredients in food processor and puree. Form mixture into 8 cakes and roll in almond bread crumb mixture. When light goes out carefully place crab cakes in hot oil. Deep-fry until golden brown, about 5 minutes. Drain on tempura rack or absorbent paper towels.

Makes: 8 cakes

Chicken with Almonds and Pineapple

Preparation time: 15 minutes
Cooking time: 45 minutes
Cooking technique: Shallow-frying, Stir-frying

⅓ cup all-purpose flour
1 teaspoon salt
¼ teaspoon pepper
3 whole chicken breasts, skinned,
   boned and cut in half
½ cup vegetable oil
½ cup slivered almonds
1 medium onion, cut in strips
1 clove garlic, minced

3 stalks celery, angle-cut into
   ¼-inch slices
2½ cups chicken broth
¼ cup soy sauce
3 tablespoons cornstarch
2 tablespoons brown sugar
1 can (20 ounces) pineapple
   chunks, with liquid

Combine flour, salt and pepper. Dredge chicken breasts in flour mixture, shaking off excess. Pour ¼ cup oil into wok. Set heat control dial at 350° F. When light goes out add almonds and stir-fry 1 minute. Remove and reserve. Add half of the chicken pieces and shallow-fry until golden brown, about 10 minutes per side. Add remaining oil if needed. When light goes out fry the remaining chicken. Remove and reserve. Add onion and garlic and stir-fry 2 minutes. Push up sides of wok. Add celery and stir-fry 3 minutes. Remove and reserve. Combine remaining ingredients except pineapple and pour mixture into wok. Simmer, stirring constantly until mixture thickens, about 1 minute. Return all cooked ingredients to wok. Add pineapple to wok. Stir to combine. Heat until hot, about 1 minute. Serve immediately with fried rice or Chinese noodles.

Makes: 6 servings

Hawaiian Chicken Velvet with Vegetables

Preparation time: 10 minutes
Cooking time: 15 minutes
Cooking technique: Stir-frying, Simmering

2½ cups chicken broth
1 tablespoon dry white wine
2 whole chicken breasts, skinned and
    boned and cut in 3-inch squares
1 small onion
1 clove garlic, crushed
1 teaspoon salt
½ teaspoon pepper

2 tablespoons vegetable oil
3 stalks celery, angle-cut into ½-inch
    slices
1 can (8 ounces)water chestnuts,
    drained and sliced
2 tablespoons cornstarch
¼ cup water

Pour broth and wine into wok. Set heat control dial at 250° F. Place chicken, onion, garlic, salt and pepper in food processor or blender and grind. Form mixture into 20 1-inch balls. When broth begins to boil add chicken balls and poach for 8 to 10 minutes. Remove and reserve chicken and broth. Wipe wok dry with paper towels. Pour oil into wok. Set heat control dial to 350° F. When light goes out add celery and water chestnuts and stir-fry 3 minutes. Remove and reserve. Combine cornstarch and water. Pour into broth and add to wok. Simmer, stirring constantly until mixture thickens, about 2 minutes. Return chicken and vegetables. Stir to combine. Heat until hot, about 2 minutes.

Makes: 4 to 6 servings

Glazed Banana Coconut Fritters

Preparation time: 10 minutes
Cooking time: 10 minutes
Cooking technique: Deep-frying

3 cups vegetable oil
1 cup all-purpose flour
2 teaspoons baking powder
1 teaspoon sugar
¼ teaspoon salt
1 egg
¼ cup coconut milk

2 teaspoons vegetable oil
2 medium-ripe bananas, mashed
¼ cup dry flaked coconut
¾ cup confectioners' sugar
⅓ cup pineapple juice
1 cup dry flaked coconut

Pour oil into wok. Set heat control dial at 425° F. While oil is heating combine flour, baking powder, sugar, and salt in a small bowl. Beat egg with coconut milk. Add 2 teaspoons oil, banana and ¼ cup coconut. Stir banana mixture into flour mixture. When light goes out drop batter by the teaspoonful into hot oil. Deep-fry until well browned, 3 to 5 minutes. While fritters are frying combine confectioners' sugar and pineapple juice. Remove fritters and drain on tempura rack or absorbent paper towels. Dip the tip of each warm fritter into glaze and then into coconut.

Makes: 36 fritters

Pork with Spinach, Hawaiian-style

Preparation time: 5 minutes
Marinating time: 1 hour
Cooking time: 35 minutes
Cooking technique: Simmering

MARINADE:

¼ cup white vinegar
1 cup chicken broth
2 teaspoons paprika
1 teaspoon salt

¼ teaspoon pepper
¼ teaspoon powdered ginger
2 tablespoons dry white wine
2 cloves garlic, minced

6 pork chops, cut ½-inch thick
¾ pound fresh spinach, cleaned,
    stems removed

In a large bowl combine marinade ingredients. Marinate chops 1 hour. Place chops with marinade into wok. Cover. Set heat control dial at 250° F. Simmer 30 minutes. Place spinach on top of chops and continue to simmer for 5 minutes. Garnish with pineapple slices and serve with buttered noodles.

Makes: 6 servings

India

India is one of the most heavily populated countries in the world. More than half of the people live in the low lying deltas, mainly because most of the food is grown in these regions. The soil is poor and crops are not plentiful enough to feed the millions who depend on them.

Farming is a major industry in India, as it must be in order to attempt to feed such a huge population. Rice is the main crop. It is generally sold rather than eaten because it brings more money than sorghum and millet, which are kept for food.

Many of the dishes of India are highly seasoned with curry, crushed red pepper, garlic and onions. Curry, which is a blend of spices is the main seasoning identified with India. In India, people grind their own spices and blend their own curries. This explains why the flavor of a standard dish can vary from town to town and household to household.

Chicken, lamb and fish are especially popular. In this section you will find many curried dishes and recipes for chutney and sautéed bananas which are delicious accompaniments to the curry flavor.

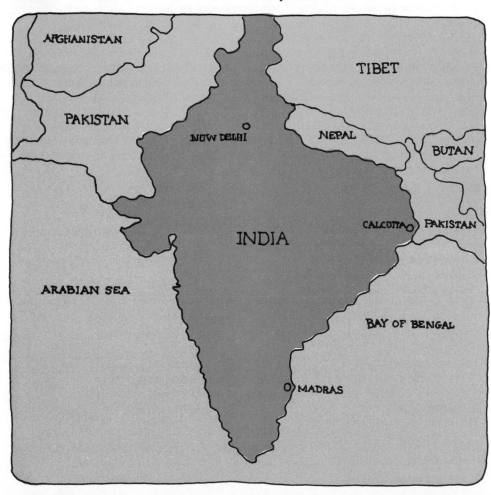

Curried Chicken

Preparation time: 20 minutes
Cooking time: 35 minutes
Cooking technique: Stewing, Simmering

1 chicken (2½ to 3 pounds)
8 cups water
2 stalks celery, cut in quarters
1 carrot, cut in quarters
1 medium onion, cut in quarters
¼ cup butter or margarine
1 medium onion, chopped
¼ pound mushrooms

2 tart cooking apples, peeled, cored
 and cut into 1-inch cubes
2 tablespoons all-purpose flour
½ teaspoon salt
⅛ teaspoon pepper
1 to 2 teaspoons curry
¾ cup milk
1 cup chicken broth

Place whole chicken in wok. Add water, celery, carrots and onions. Set heat control dial at 250° F. Cover. Simmer chicken for 20 minutes. Turn chicken over and simmer for 20 minutes longer. Remove and cool completely. Strain stock and reserve. Discard vegetables. Wipe wok clean with paper towel. Remove chicken from bones and cut into 1-inch chunks. Discard skin and bones. Reserve chicken. Set heat control dial at 250° F. Add butter and when it starts to melt (do not wait for light to go out) add onions and sauté for 5 minutes or until transparent. Push up sides of wok. Add mushrooms and sauté for 30 seconds. Push up sides of wok. Add butter if needed. When light goes out sauté apples for 2 minutes. Remove all ingredients and reserve. Combine remaining ingredients and pour mixture into wok. Simmer, stirring constantly until mixture thickens, about 5 minutes. Return chicken and all other ingredients to wok. Stir well to combine. Heat until hot, about 1 minute. Serve immediately over rice. Serve with chutney, chopped peanuts, coconut, chopped onions, and sautéed bananas as toppings.

Makes: 8 servings

Chutney

Preparation time: 15 minutes
Cooking time: 1 hour 30 minutes
Cooking technique: Simmering

1 cup white vinegar
1 cup brown sugar
½ cup white sugar
1 teaspoon salt
½ teaspoon dried crushed red
 pepper
½ teaspoon allspice
½ teaspoon powdered ginger

2 cloves garlic, minced
6 apples, peeled, cored
 and diced
½ pound dried prunes
½ pound dried apricots
1 cup raisins
½ cup orange juice

Place all ingredients in wok. Set heat control dial at 225° F. Cover. Simmer for 1½ hours, stirring occasionally.

Makes: 4 cups

Recipes - India

Ground Lamb Curry

Preparation time: 5 minutes
Cooking time: 10 minutes
Cooking technique: Sautéeing

2 tablespoons butter
1 large onion, chopped
6 mushrooms, sliced
1 pound ground lamb
1 teaspoon salt

¼ teaspoon pepper
½ teaspoon curry
⅛ to ¼ teaspoon ground coriander
¼ teaspoon crushed red pepper
¼ cup plain yogurt

Place butter in wok. Set heat control dial at 350° F. When butter melts (do not wait for light to go out), add onion and sauté 2 minutes. Add mushrooms and sauté 1 minute. Push up sides of wok. Add lamb and seasonings and sauté 3 to 5 minutes until meat is cooked. Stir in onions, mushrooms and yogurt and simmer for 2 minutes.

Makes: 4 servings

Sautéed Bananas and Mandarin Oranges

Preparation time: 5 minutes
Cooking time: 5 minutes
Cooking technique: Sautéeing

3 tablespoons butter
4 bananas, cut in ½-inch rounds
1 can (11 ounces) mandarin orange
  segments, drained

2 tablespoons brown sugar
⅛ teaspoon cinnamon
⅛ teaspoon nutmeg
2 teaspoons almond flavored liqueur

Place butter in wok. Set heat control dial at 250° F. When butter begins to melt (do not wait for light to go out), add bananas and sauté for 1 minute. Add remaining ingredients and simmer uncovered for 2 minutes, stirring occasionally. Serve with curried dishes.

Makes: 4 servings

Chicken *Tandori*

Preparation time: 15 minutes
Cooking time: 40 minutes
Cooking technique: Shallow-frying, Simmering

¼ cup vegetable oil
1 chicken (2½ to 3 pounds), cut
   in pieces
1 medium onion, chopped
2 stalks celery, chopped
1 green pepper, chopped
1 clove garlic, minced
1 tomato, chopped

1 cup chicken broth
1 teaspoon salt
¼ teaspoon pepper
1 to 2 teaspoons curry
¼ to ½ teaspoon crushed coriander
¼ to ½ teaspoon turmeric
¼ teaspoon cinnamon

Pour oil into wok. Set heat control dial at 350° F. When light goes out add chicken and brown well on all sides, about 15 minutes. Remove and reserve. Add onions and sauté until lightly browned, about 2 minutes. Push up sides of wok. Add celery and green peppers and sauté 2 minutes. Push up sides of wok. Add garlic and tomato and sauté 1 minute. Combine broth and seasonings and pour into wok. Stir in all ingredients and combine. Return chicken and cover. Turn heat control dial to 250° F. Simmer 20 minutes. Serve with rice and chutney.

Makes: 4 servings

Mulligatawny Soup

Preparation time: 20 minutes
Cooking time: 40 minutes
Cooking technique: Stewing

1 chicken (2½ to 3 pounds) cut
   in pieces
6 cups water
1 teaspoon salt
¼ teaspoon pepper
1 to 2 teaspoons curry
¼ teaspoon turmeric

1 large onion, chopped
3 stalks celery, chopped
3 carrots, chopped
2 teaspoons chopped parsley
¾ cup raw rice
½ cup heavy cream

Place the chicken, water, salt, pepper, curry and turmeric into wok. Cover. Set heat control dial at 250° F. Simmer for 15 minutes. Add vegetables and rice. Cover. Simmer for 20 minutes. Stir in cream. Serve immediately.

Makes: 6 servings

Recipes
From the West

The non-oriental recipes in this section include Mexican, French, Spanish, Italian, and American favorites. Here you'll discover just a few of the many ways to use your wok for western foods. Try some of the soups, main dishes, vegetables and desserts, and you will see how easy it can be to adapt your own special recipe for preparation in the wok.

And...
Donuts, candies, crêpes, omelets and fondue are other culinary delights to be found here. Your wok can really demonstrate its versatility with these recipes where East meets West...in your wok!

Appetizers

Swedish Meatballs

Preparation time: 15 minutes
Cooking time: 40 minutes
Cooking technique: Shallow-frying, Simmering

MEATBALL MIXTURE:

1 pound ground beef
½ pound ground pork
½ pound ground veal
2 eggs
1 clove garlic, minced
1 medium onion, finely chopped
½ cup vegetable oil

¾ cup dried flavored
   bread crumbs
⅓ cup milk
1 teaspoon salt
⅛ teaspoon pepper
½ teaspoon dried dill weed

SAUCE:

1 can (10½ ounces) condensed
   cream of mushroom soup, undiluted
2 cups beef broth

In a large bowl, combine meatball mixture. Form into 48 (1-inch) meatballs. Pour oil into wok. Set heat control dial at 350° F. When light goes out, add one-half of the meatballs and shallow-fry until well browned on all sides, about 5 minutes. Remove and drain on tempura rack or absorbent paper towels. When light goes out, add remaining meatballs and fry until brown.

Turn heat control dial to "off." Carefully discard oil. Wipe wok clean with paper towel. Add sauce ingredients. Turn heat control dial to 225° F. Stir well until mushroom soup is dissolved. When light goes out add meatballs and simmer for 30 minutes. Turn heat control dial to "serve" and serve with toothpicks as an hors d'oeuvre, or use as a main dish with buttered noodles.

Makes: 48 (1-inch) meatballs

Fried Shrimp

Preparation time: 30 minutes
Cooking time: 5 minutes
Cooking technique: Deep-frying

¾ pound uncooked medium-sized
shrimp, peeled (leave on tails) and
deveined
1 egg, slightly beaten
1 can (3 ounces) chow mein noodles,
finely crushed

1 clove garlic, very finely minced
½ small onion, very finely minced
3 cups vegetable oil
Dipping Sauce
Ginger Sauce

Pour oil into wok. Set heat control dial at 425° F. While oil is heating dip each shrimp into beaten egg. Combine noodles, garlic and onion. Roll shrimp in the mixture. When light goes out, carefully drop about half of the shrimp into the hot oil. Fry until golden brown, about 2 to 3 minutes. Drain on tempura rack or absorbent paper towels. Continue to fry shrimp until they are all done. Serve with Dipping Sauce, or Ginger Sauce.

Makes: About 30 appetizers

Dipping Sauce

4 tablespoons dry mustard
3 or 4 tablespoons water
1 cup soy sauce

In a small bowl, add enough of the water to the mustard to make a smooth paste. Blend in the soy sauce.

Makes: 1 cup

Ginger Sauce

1 tablespoon ground ginger
1 clove garlic, crushed
½ cup water

¼ cup sugar
1 cup soy sauce

Blend all ingredients in a small bowl.

Makes: 1 cup

Cheese Balls

Preparation time: 10 minutes
Cooking time: 5 minutes
Cooking technique: Deep-frying

8 ounces Cheddar cheese, shredded
2 tablespoons all-purpose flour
2 tablespoons very finely chopped
   onions
½ teaspoon garlic salt
¼ teaspoon pepper
2 egg whites
3 cups vegetable oil

In a small bowl combine cheese, flour, onion, garlic salt and pepper. Beat egg whites until they form stiff, not dry peaks. Fold beaten egg white into the cheese mixture. Pour oil into wok. Set heat control dial at 425° F. Form into 30 (1-inch) balls. When light goes out, add one half of the cheese balls and fry until brown, about 2 minutes. Drain on tempura rack or absorbent paper. Serve warm with toothpicks.

Makes: 30

Soups

Split Pea Soup

Preparation time: 15 minutes
Cooking time: 1 hour 30 minutes
Cooking technique: Sautéeing, Simmering

1 tablespoon vegetable oil	3 chicken boullion cubes
1 onion, finely chopped	1 pound dried green split peas
1 carrot, finely chopped	1 teaspoon salt
1 clove garlic, minced	½ teaspoon pepper
10 cups water	6 hot dogs, cut in 1-inch pieces

Pour oil into wok. Set heat control dial at 300° F. When light goes out add onion, carrot and garlic. Sauté for 2 minutes. Add water, boullion cubes, peas, salt and pepper. Stir. Allow liquid to come to a boil then turn heat control dial to 225° F. and cook covered for 2 hours, stirring occasionally. Add hot dogs and continue to simmer uncovered for 30 minutes. Serve with crackers or croutons.

Makes: 4 to 6 servings

Basic Stock

Preparation time: 10 minutes
Cooking time: 2 to 3 hours
Cooking technique: Simmering

12 cups water	1 onion, cut in quarters
1 pound beef bones or chicken backs and necks	1 medium tomato, cut in quarters
1 large carrot, scraped and cut in quarters	3 beef or chicken boullion cubes
1 cup celery leaves and tops	1 teaspoon salt
	¼ teaspoon pepper

Place all ingredients in wok. Set heat control dial at 250° F. Cover. Simmer for 2 to 3 hours. Strain liquid and discard vegetables and bones. Use in recipes that call for stock or broth.

Makes: 8 cups

New England Clam Chowder

Preparation time: 20 minutes
Cooking time: 20 minutes
Cooking technique: Sautéeing, Simmering

¼ pound bacon, cut in 1-inch pieces
3 potatoes, diced

2 medium onions, chopped
4 stalks celery, sliced

2 tablespoons butter
2 tablespoons all-purpose flour
2 cups milk
2 teaspoons salt

¼ to ½ teaspoon pepper
2 cans (6½ ounces each) minced
   clams with liquid

Place bacon in wok. Set heat control dial at 300° F. Fry bacon until crisp, about 5 minutes. While bacon is frying cut vegetables. Remove bacon and crumble into bits to garnish soup. Sauté potatoes in hot bacon fat for 3 to 5 minutes. Add onions and continue to sauté for 3 minutes. Add celery and sauté 2 to 3 minutes longer. When all vegetables are lightly browned or tender remove and reserve. Turn heat control dial to 250° F. Melt butter and add flour stirring until mixture forms a paste. Pour milk and add salt and pepper to mixture stirring constantly until mixture thickens. Return vegetables to wok and simmer with sauce for 5 minutes. Stir in clams with their liquid and heat 2 minutes. Garnish with crumbled bacon.

Makes: 6 cups

Corn Chowder

Preparation time: 10 minutes
Cooking time: 25 minutes
Cooking technique: Sautéeing, Simmering

¼ pound bacon, cut in 1-inch strips
1 medium onion, chopped
1½ cups thinly sliced celery
6 cups corn, cut from cob (8 to 10
   ears), or 3 cans (1 pound each)
   whole kernel corn, drained

2 cups chicken broth
1 can (13 ounces) evaporated milk
1 teaspoon salt
½ teaspoon pepper

Place bacon in wok. Set heat control dial at 300° F. Fry bacon until crisp, about 5 minutes. While bacon is frying prepare all ingredients. Remove bacon and crumble into bits for garnish. Discard all but 2 tablespoons of bacon fat. Add onion and celery and sauté until lightly browned, about 3 minutes. Add remaining ingredients to wok. Bring to a boil. Cover. Turn heat control dial to 225° F. Simmer for 20 minutes. Garnish soup with bacon bits.

Makes: 8 cups

Main Dishes

Meatballs in Bordelaise Sauce

Preparation time: 30 minutes
Cooking time: 1 hour, 45 minutes
Cooking technique: Shallow-frying

2 tablespoons vegetable oil
1 onion, chopped
1 clove garlic, chopped
2 carrots, chopped
1 can (10¾ ounces) beef broth
1 cup dry red wine
1½ cups water
2 teaspons browning sauce
1 pound ground beef
1 egg

½ cup dried flavored bread
  crumbs
¼ cup milk
1 teaspoon salt
¼ teaspoon pepper
¼ cup vegetable oil
½ pound mushrooms, cleaned
  and sliced
1 tablespoon flour
¼ cup water

Pour oil into wok. Set heat control dial at 350° F. When light goes out add onions, garlic and carrots and sauté 2 minutes. Add broth, wine, water and browning sauce. Stir. Allow liquid to come to a boil. When mixture boils, turn heat control to 225° F. and simmer uncovered for 45 minutes or until sauce is reduced by half. While sauce is simmering prepare meatballs.

    Combine ground beef, egg, bread crumbs, milk, salt and pepper, mixing well. Form mixture into 30 (1-inch) meatballs. When sauce is reduced, turn heat control dial to "off." Pour sauce through a strainer into a large bowl. Press all liquid from vegetables and discard vegetables. Wipe wok clean with a paper towel. Pour oil into wok. Set heat control dial at 350° F. When light goes out add meatballs, brown well on both sides. Remove meatballs to bowl with sauce. Add mushrooms to wok and sauté 1 minute. Remove mushrooms to bowl with meatballs and sauce. Turn heat control to "off." Carefully discard oil. Wipe wok clean with a paper towel. Combine flour and water making a paste and pour into wok. Return all ingredients to wok. Set heat control dial at 225° F. and simmer 30 minutes, stirring occasionally. Serve over buttered noodles.

Makes: 4 servings

Turkey Croquettes

Preparation time: 10 minutes
Cooking time: 20 minutes
Cooking technique: Deep-frying

3 cups vegetable oil
½ pound cooked turkey, cut in cubes
2 small boiled potatoes
4 mushrooms
1 carrot, cut in chucks
1 stalk celery
1 egg

6 slices bread
¼ cup milk
1 teaspoon salt
¼ teaspoon pepper
3 tablespoons all-purpose flour
½ cup flavored dried bread
    crumbs

Pour oil into wok. Set heat control dial at 425° F. Place all ingredients except flavored bread crumbs into food processor or blender and puree. Form mixture into 24 (3-inch) ovals. Roll in bread crumbs. When light goes out carefully place 8 croquettes in wok. Deep-fry until well browned, about 3 to 5 minutes. Continue until all croquettes are fried. Drain on tempura rack or absorbent paper towels. Serve with turkey gravy or cheese sauce.

Makes: 12

Beer-batter Dipped Chicken

Preparation time: 10 minutes
Cooking time: 40 minutes
Cooking technique: Deep-frying

3 cups vegetable oil
2 cups biscuit mix
1 egg
½ cup beer
1 cup club soda

2 teaspoons salt
¼ teaspoon pepper
3 whole chicken breasts, skinned,
    boned and cut in 2-inch strips

Pour oil into wok. Set heat control dial at 425° F. While oil is heating, combine biscuit mix, egg, beer, club soda, salt and pepper. Dip chicken slices into batter. When light goes out carefully place 4 or 5 pieces of chicken into oil. Deep-fry until golden brown, about 5 to 8 minutes. Drain on tempura rack or absorbent paper towels. Continue to fry until all chicken is cooked.

Makes: 6 servings

Variation I: Substitute 2 pounds flounder or sole fish filets for chicken. Add ½ teaspoon dill, ½ teaspoon basil and 1 tablespoon dried chopped chives to batter.

Variation II: Substitute eggplant, zucchini, cauliflower or onions for chicken. Dredge vegetables in flour before dipping in batter.

Beef and Beer

Preparation time: 20 minutes
Cooking time: 2 hours 30 minutes
Cooking technique: Sautéeing, Simmering

¼ cup oil
2 large onions, thinly sliced
3½ pounds stewing beef, cut in
   1-inch cubes
2 cups beef broth
1 can (12 ounces) beer
2 cups shredded Cheddar cheese
2 teaspoons browning and seasoning sauce

1 tablespoon brown sugar
¼ teaspoon tarragon
¼ teaspoon thyme
½ teaspoon salt
¼ teaspoon pepper
½ cup water
3 tablespoons cornstarch

Pour oil into wok. Set heat control dial at 350° F. When light goes out add onions
and sauté until golden brown, about 5 minutes. Remove and reserve. Add ⅓ of meat
at a time and brown well on all sides, about 10 minutes. Remove and reserve. Continue to fry until all meat is cooked. Return onions to wok. Add broth, beer, cheese,
browning sauce, sugar and spices. Stir well to combine. Cover. Turn heat control
dial to 250° F. Simmer for 1½ hours. Combine water and cornstarch and pour into
wok. Stir well to combine. Simmer, stirring occasionally until mixture thickens, about
2 minutes.

Makes: 6 to 8 servings

Chicken Scallops *Marengo*

Preparation time: 15 minutes
Cooking time: 45 minutes
Cooking technique: Sautéeing

½ cup all-purpose flour
1 teaspoon salt
¼ teaspoon pepper
½ teaspoon paprika
½ teaspoon poultry seasoning
4 whole chicken breasts, skinned,
   boned and cut into 1-inch pieces
½ cup butter or margarine
1 medium onion, chopped

¼ pound mushrooms, sliced
1 can (10¾ ounces) cream of celery
   soup, undiluted
2 tablespoons catsup
1 cup chicken broth
¼ cup dry red wine
1 can (1 pound) whole boiled onions,
   drained

Combine flour and seasonings. Dredge chicken pieces in flour, shaking off excess.
Place butter in wok. Set heat control dial at 300° F. When butter melts (do not wait
for light to go out) add chicken and sauté until lightly browned, about 5 minutes per
side. Remove and reserve. When light goes out add onions and sauté until lightly
browned, about 3 minutes. Add mushrooms and sauté 1 minute. Add remaining ingredients and return chicken to wok. Stir well to combine. Turn heat control dial to
250° F. Simmer for 15 minutes and serve.

Makes: 6 to 8 servings

Beef and Vegetables *Pizziola*

Preparation time: 20 minutes
Cooking time: 40 minutes
Cooking technique: Sautéeing, Simmering

⅓ cup vegetable oil
2 pounds boneless sirlion steak, cut
  in 1-inch pieces
3 large cloves garlic, crushed
1 large onion, chopped
1 large green pepper, diced
2 large zucchini, sliced
1 can (1 pound 12 ounces) concen-
  trated crushed tomatoes

1 tablespoon freshly chopped
  parsley
1 teaspoon basil
1 teaspoon oregano
1 teaspoon salt
1 tablespoon sugar
¼ teaspoon pepper
1 teaspoon browning and seasoning
  sauce
¼ cup dry white wine

Pour 2 tablespoons oil into wok. Set heat control dial at 350° F. Add steak 6 to 8 pieces at at time. Brown well, about 2 minutes per side. Continue until all meat is cooked. Add oil as needed. Remove and reserve. Add remaining oil. When light goes out add garlic and onion and sauté until lightly browned, about 1 minute. Push up sides of wok. Add green pepper and sauté 3 minutes or until tender. Push up sides of wok. Add zucchini and sauté until lightly browned, about 3 minutes. Return vegetables to wok. Add remaining ingredients and stir well to combine. Turn heat control dial to 250° F. Simmer uncovered for 10 minutes. Return meat to wok. Stir well to combine. Heat 1 minute and serve with noodles or spaghetti.

Makes: 6 to 8 servings

Beef Stroganoff

Preparation time: 20 minutes
Cooking time: 15 minutes
Cooking technique: Sautéeing

⅓ cup butter or margarine
½ cup onion, minced
1 pound flank steak, angle-cut
   into thin slices
¾ pound mushrooms, thinly sliced
2½ cups beef broth
¼ cup dry red wine

1 teaspoon salt
¼ teaspoon pepper
¼ cup all-purpose flour
1 cup sour cream
¼ teaspoon dill
1 teaspoon chives

Place ¼ cup butter into wok. Set heat control dial at 250° F. When butter melts (do not wait for light to go out) sauté onions until transparent, about 4 minutes. Push up sides of wok. Add beef and brown for 2 minutes. Add remaining butter. When light goes out add mushrooms and sauté 1 minute. Combine broth, wine, salt, pepper and flour. Pour into wok. Add onions from side of wok. Simmer, stirring constantly until mixture thickens, about 3 minutes. Combine sour cream, dill and chives. Spoon into wok. Stir well to combine. Heat until hot, about 30 seconds. Serve immediately over buttered noodles.

Makes: 4 to 6 servings

Potato, Ham and Egg Hash

Preparation time: 15 minutes
Cooking time: 15 minutes
Cooking technique: Sautéeing and Steaming

½ cup vegetable oil
2 medium potatoes, cut in
   ½-inch cubes
1 large onion
¼ pound ham, chopped
6 mushrooms, sliced

¼ teaspoon salt
⅛ teaspoon pepper
¼ teaspoon garlic powder
6 eggs
3 tablespoons milk

Pour oil into wok. Set heat control dial at 300° F. Add potatoes and sauté for 15 minutes or until lightly browned. Add onions and sauté 3 minutes. Push up sides of wok. Add ham and mushrooms and sauté 1 minute. Add seasonings and stir well. Turn heat control dial to 225° F. Cover. Allow mixture to steam until potatoes are tender, about 3 minutes. While potatoes are steaming combine eggs and milk. Pour eggs into wok. Stir in potatoes and stir constantly until eggs are set, about 2 minutes.

Makes: 4 servings

Calzone

Preparation time: 15 minutes
Rising time: 1 hour
Cooking time: 20 minutes
Cooking technique: Deep-frying

1 package (¼ ounce) active dry yeast
1¼ cups warm water
¼ teaspoon sugar
3¼ to 3½ cups all-purpose flour
1 teaspoon salt
¼ teaspoon pepper
1 pound ricotta cheese
¼ pound mozzarella cheese

2 tablespoons grated Parmesan cheese
1 egg
¼ teaspoon basil
½ teaspoon parsley
¼ teaspoon garlic salt
3½ cups vegetable oil

In a small bowl dissolve yeast in ¼ cup warm water. Stir in sugar. Allow to rise in a warm dark place for 5 to 10 minutes or until yeast bubbles and grows. If it does not grow, yeast is dead. Start again. In a large bowl mix yeast mixture, remaining water, flour, salt and pepper. Turn dough onto a lightly floured board. Knead until shiny and elastic, about 5 to 7 minutes. Place dough in a lightly oiled bowl. Cover. Place in a warm draft free place to rise until doubled in bulk, about 1 hour. Combine remaining ingredients except oil and reserve for filling. Pour oil into wok. Set heat control dial at 425° F. While oil is heating divide dough into 8 equal sized pieces. Roll each piece of dough into a 4-inch circle. Place about ¼ cup of filling mixture into the center of each circle and crimp edges. When light goes out fry 4 calzones at a time until golden brown, about 3 to 5 minutes on each side. Drain on tempura rack or absorbent paper towels.

Makes: 8

Chicken and Rice

Preparation time: 10 minutes
Cooking time: 1 hour 15 minutes
Cooking technique: Shallow-frying, Steaming

½ cup vegetable oil
⅓ cup all-purpose flour
1 teaspoon salt
⅛ teaspoon pepper
1 chicken (2½ to 3 pounds)
 cut in pieces
1 medium onion, chopped
2 stalks celery, chopped

1 cup long grain rice, uncooked
2½ cups chicken broth
½ cup water
¼ cup soy sauce
⅓ cup Sweet and Sour Sauce
1 teaspoon salt
¼ teaspoon pepper

Pour oil into wok. Set heat control dial at 350° F. Combine flour, salt and pepper. Dredge chicken in flour, shaking off excess. When light goes out, shallow-fry 4 or 5 pieces of chicken at a time until golden brown, about 20 minutes. Remove and re-serve. Add onions and celery and sauté 3 to 5 minutes or until lightly browned. Add rice and sauté 1 minute. Add all the remaining ingredients and stir well to combine. Cover. Turn heat control dial to 225° F. Steam for 10 minutes. Place chicken on top of rice. Cover. Steam 10 to 15 minutes or until rice is tender.

Makes: 6 servings

Lemon Chicken

Preparation time: 10 minutes
Cooking time: 40 minutes
Cooking technique: Shallow-frying, Sautéeing, Simmering

¾ cup vegetable oil
3 whole chicken breasts, skinned,
 boned and cut in half
⅓ cup all-purpose flour

1 egg
¼ cup milk
¾ cup flavored dried bread crumbs

2 medium onions, sliced
½ pound mushrooms, sliced
1 teaspoon salt
¼ teaspoon pepper
2½ cups chicken broth

¼ cup dry white wine
2 teaspoons browning sauce
3 tablespoons all-purpose flour
Juice of ½ lemon or 1 tablespoon
 reconstituted lemon juice

Pour ½ cup vegetable oil into wok. Set heat control dial at 350° F. Flatten chicken and dredge in flour, shaking off excess. Combine egg and milk. Dip chicken in egg-milk mixture and then roll in bread crumbs. When light goes out shallow-fry chicken until well browned, about 5 to 8 minutes per side. Remove and reserve. Add remaining oil. When light goes out sauté onions until browned, about 3 minutes. Add mushrooms and sauté 1 minute. Remove and reserve. Combine remaining ingredients. Pour mixture into wok. Simmer, stirring constantly until mixture thickens, about 1 minute. Return all ingredients to wok. Stir well to combine. Simmer uncovered for 10 to 15 minutes. Serve with noodles or home-fried potatoes.

Makes: 6 servings

Hungarian Goulash

Preparation time: 20 minutes
Cooking time: 2 hours
Cooking technique: Sautéeing, Simmering

¼ cup butter or margarine
4 medium onions, cut in strips
1 cup all-purpose flour
1 teaspoon salt
¼ teaspoon pepper
2 pounds beef, rump or bottom
　round, cut in 1-inch cubes
½ cup vegetable oil

1 tablespoon paprika
1 teaspoon salt
¼ teaspoon pepper
2 tablespoons catsup
1 teaspoon browning and seasoning
　sauce
2½ cups beef broth
¾ cup red wine

Place butter in wok. Set heat control dial at 350° F. As soon as butter begins to melt (do not wait for light to go out), add onions and sauté until golden brown. Remove and reserve. Combine flour, salt and pepper in a plastic bag. Add meat and shake well to coat. Pour oil into wok. When light goes out add half of the meat and brown well on all sides, about 6 to 8 minutes. Remove and reserve. Continue until all meat is browned. Add reserved onions and meat to wok. Combine remaining ingredients and add to wok. Stir well to combine. Cover. Turn heat control dial to 250° F. Simmer 1 hour 30 minutes, stirring occasionally.

Makes: 6 to 8 servings

Chili

Preparation time: 5 minutes
Cooking time: 1 hour 50 minutes
Cooking technique: Shallow-frying, Simmering

½ cup vegetable oil
1 cup all-purpose flour
1 teaspoon salt
¼ teaspoon pepper
2 pounds stewing beef, cut in
　1-inch cubes
1 large onion, chopped
2 cloves garlic, minced

1 can (1 pound 12 ounces) whole
　tomatoes in puree
¼ cup red wine
3 teaspoons chili powder
¼ teaspoon crushed red pepper
1 teaspoon paprika
½ teaspoon cumin seeds

Pour ¼ cup oil into wok. Set heat control dial at 350° F. Combine flour, salt and pepper in a plastic bag and add meat. Shake to coat. When light goes out add half of the meat. Shallow-fry until browned on all sides, about 6 to 8 minutes. Remove and reserve. Add remaining oil and the rest of the meat. Shallow-fry as before. Remove and reserve. Add onions and garlic and sauté 1 minute. Combine remaining ingredients and pour into wok. Return meat and stir well to combine. Cover. Turn heat control dial to 250° F. Simmer until meat is tender, about 2 hours.

Makes: 6 to 8 servings

Fried Fish with Hush Puppies

Preparation time: 25 minutes
Cooking time: 10 minutes
Cooking technique: Deep-frying

2 pounds fish fillets, fresh or frozen,
   thawed
3 tablespoons lemon juice
3 cups vegetable oil
1 egg, beaten
¼ cup milk

1 teaspoon salt
⅛ teaspoon pepper
1¼ cups flavored, dry bread crumbs
Hush Puppies
Tartar Sauce

Sprinkle fish with lemon juice and let stand 15 minutes. Pour oil into wok. Set heat control dial at 425° F. While oil is heating, combine egg, milk, salt and pepper. Dip fish in egg mixture and then into crumbs. When light goes out, fry 4 slices at a time until golden brown, about 3 to 5 minutes. Continue to fry until all fish is fried. Drain on tempura rack or absorbent paper towels. Serve with Hush Puppies and Tartar Sauce.

Makes: 6 servings

Hush Puppies

Preparation time: 10 minutes
Cooking time: 15 minutes
Cooking technique: Deep-frying

3 cups vegetable oil
1½ cups white cornmeal
½ cup all-purpose flour
2½ teaspoons baking powder
1 teaspoon salt

½ teaspoon garlic powder
¼ teaspoon pepper
1 medium onion, finely chopped
½ cup milk
1 egg, beaten

Pour oil into wok. Set heat control dial at 425° F. While oil is heating, combine dry ingredients in a medium-sized bowl. Add remaining ingredients and stir only until blended. When light goes out, drop batter by tablespoonfuls into wok and fry for 3 to 4 minutes or until well browned. Drain on tempura rack or absorbent paper towels.

Makes: 18 Hush Puppies

Fishburgers

Preparation time: 10 minutes
Cooking time: 20 minutes
Cooking technique: Simmering, Shallow-frying

1½ pounds fish fillets,
  fresh or frozen, thawed
1 quart water
1 teaspoon salt
3 eggs, beaten
¼ cup grated Parmesan cheese
1 tablespoon chopped parsley

1 clove garlic, finely chopped
½ teaspoon salt
⅛ teaspoon pepper
½ cup dry, flavored bread crumbs
2 cups cornflakes, very finely crushed
¾ cup vegetable oil

6 toasted sesame seed rolls
Tartar Sauce

Pour water into wok. Place fish in wok. Set heat control dial at 225° F. Cover wok and simmer for 8 to 10 minutes. Drain. Wipe wok dry with paper towel. Combine eggs, cheese, parsley, garlic, salt, pepper, bread crumbs and fish. Shape into 6 patties and roll in cornflake crumbs. Set heat control dial at 350° F.; add vegetable oil. When light goes out, place patties in wok; fry until brown on one side, about 5 minutes. Turn carefully and brown the other side. Drain on tempura rack or absorbent paper.

Place each fishburger on bottom half of roll. Top with Tartar Sauce and top half of roll.

Makes: 6 servings

Tarragon Fried Fish

Preparation time: 10 minutes
Cooking time: 10 minutes
Cooking technique: Shallow-frying

½ cup cornmeal
½ cup all-purpose flour
2 teaspoons onion salt
½ teaspoon salt
¼ teaspoon pepper
¼ teaspoon crushed tarragon

½ cup vegetable oil
2 pounds fish fillets, fresh or frozen,
  thawed
½ cup tarragon vinegar
Lemon wedges

Combine cornmeal, flour and seasonings. Pour oil into wok. Set heat control dial at 350° F. While oil is heating, dip fish in vinegar and then into cornmeal mixture. When light goes out, shallow-fry 3 or 4 pieces at a time until brown on both sides, 3 to 4 minutes per side. Drain on tempura rack or absorbent paper towels. Serve with lemon wedges.

Makes: 6 servings

Crispy Scallops

Preparation time: 10 minutes
Cooking time: 15 minutes
Cooking technique: Deep-frying

3 cups vegetable oil
¾ cup catsup
1 tablespoon mustard
1 tablespoon lemon juice
1 pound bay scallops, or other fish
   cut in bite-size pieces

1¼ cups all-purpose flour
½ cup dried bread crumbs
Cocktail Sauce
Lemon wedges

Pour oil into wok. Set heat control dial at 425° F. While oil is heating, combine catsup, mustard and lemon juice in a large bowl. Add scallops and stir well to coat. In a shallow baking dish combine flour and bread crumbs. With a slotted spoon, remove scallops from bowl and dredge in flour/crumb mixture. Toss well to coat. When light goes out place about one-third of the scallops into wok. Deep-fry until golden brown, about 2 to 3 minutes. Drain on absorbent paper towels. Continue as above until all scallops are fried. Serve with cocktail sauce and lemon wedges.

Makes: 4 servings

Spanish Rice

Preparation time: 15 minutes
Cooking time: 35 to 40 minutes
Cooking technique: Sautéeing, Simmering

¼ pound bacon, chopped
1 large onion, chopped
1 large green pepper, chopped
1 clove garlic, finely chopped
2 cups water
1 can (1 pound 12 ounces) crushed
   tomatoes

¾ cup uncooked rice
1 tablespoon chopped parsley
1 teaspoon salt
¼ teaspoon black pepper
¼ teaspoon dried crushed red
   pepper
1 teaspoon sugar

Place bacon in wok. Set heat control dial at 300° F. Sauté bacon until crisp, about 6 minutes. Push up sides of wok. Add onion, green pepper and garlic, and sauté until tender, about 2 minutes. Add remaining ingredients. Stir well to combine. Turn heat control dial to 250° F. Cover and simmer for 25 to 30 minutes, or until rice is tender. Stir well before serving to allow rice to absorb any remaining liquid.

Makes: 6 (1 cup) servings

Cheese Fondue

Preparation time: 20 minutes
Cooking time: 5 minutes
Cooking technique: Simmering

1 tablespoon butter
½ small onion, finely minced
1 clove garlic, finely minced
1 teaspoon cornstarch
¾ cup dry white wine
¼ cup chicken broth
¾ pound Swiss cheese, grated
¾ pound Cheddar cheese, grated

1 teaspoon sugar
¼ teaspoon pepper
Pinch dill
Pinch basil
Pinch paprika
1 large loaf French bread, cut
 in 1-inch chunks

Place butter into wok. Set heat control dial at 250° F. As soon as butter begins to melt (do not wait for light to go out) add onion and garlic. Sauté until onions are limp, about 2 minutes. Dissolve cornstarch in wine and stir into wok. Add remaining ingredients except bread and simmer for 5 minutes, stirring occasionally during serving. Add additional broth or wine if fondue becomes too thick. Spear bread cubes with long handled fondue forks. Dip bread into fondue and swirl to coat.

Makes: 8 servings

Sauces

Tomato Sauce

Preparation time: 20 minutes
Cooking time: 2 to 3 hours
Cooking technique: Sautéeing, Simmering

3 tablespoons vegetable oil
1 pound pork sausage
2 large onions, chopped
2 cloves garlic, crushed
2 cans (1 pound 12 ounces each)
   whole tomatoes, pureed

3 cans (6 ounces each) tomato paste
8 cups water
1 teaspoon basil
1 teaspoon parsley flakes
2 teaspoons salt
2 tablespoons sugar

Pour oil into wok. Set heat control dial at 300° F. When light goes out brown sausage for 5 minutes. Add onions and garlic and sauté until browned, about 2 minutes. Add remaining ingredients. Stir well to combine. Cover. Turn heat control dial to 250° F. and simmer 2 to 3 hours stirring occasionally.

Makes: 4 quarts

Anchovy Sauce

Preparation time: 10 minutes
Cooking time: 25 minutes
Cooking technique: Sautéeing, Simmering

2 tablespoons vegetable oil
2 cloves garlic, crushed
1 medium onion, chopped
2 cans (2 ounces each) anchovies,
   drained
6 cups tomato sauce
2 tablespoons freshly chopped
   parsley or ½ teaspoon dried
   parsley

2 tablespoons dry red wine
¼ teaspoon pepper
½ teaspoon basil
½ teaspoon oregano
1 can (3½ ounces) pitted black
   olives, drained and sliced

Pour oil into wok. Set heat control dial at 300° F. When light goes out add garlic and onions. Sauté until lightly browned, about 2 minutes. Add anchovies and cook, stirring until anchovies are dissolved into a paste, about 2 minutes. Add tomato sauce, wine and herbs. Cover. Turn heat control dial to 225° F. Simmer 20 minutes. Stir in olives and cook 1 minute. Serve over cooked spaghetti.

Makes: 6 (½ cup) servings

Vegetables

Cauliflower with Cheese Sauce

Preparation time: 10 minutes
Cooking time: 15 minutes
Cooking technique: Steaming

2 cups water
1 head (1 pound) cauliflower,
   trimmed and whole
1 cup milk
1 tablespoon grated Parmesan
   cheese
1 teaspoon salt

1 teaspoon mustard
¼ teaspoon dill
¼ teaspoon pepper
2 tablespoons butter
2 tablespoons all-purpose flour
¼ pound Cheddar cheese, grated

Place steamer insert or rack into wok. Pour water into wok. Place whole cauliflower on steamer insert. Set heat control dial at 250° F. Cover. Steam for 12 to 15 minutes or until tender. While cauliflower is steaming, prepare sauce ingredients by combining milk, Parmesan cheese and seasonings. Remove cauliflower to covered serving bowl to keep warm. Drain wok. Melt butter, add flour, stirring until mixture forms a paste. Pour milk mixture into wok stirring constantly until sauce thickens. Add Cheddar cheese and stir well, until cheese melts. Pour cheese sauce over cauliflower and serve immediately.

Makes: 6 servings

Deep-fried Potato Skins

Preparation time: 5 minutes
Cooking time: 20 minutes
Cooking technique: Deep-frying

6 potatoes
3 cups vegetable oil
½ cup milk
2 tablespoons butter

2 tablespoons cream cheese or
    Cheddar cheese spread
½ teaspoon salt
⅛ teaspoon pepper

Bake potatoes until fork tender, about 40 minutes. Pour oil into wok. Set heat control dial at 425° F. Scoop out inside of potatoes being careful not to break skins. Leave a thin layer of potato on skin if complete removal will cause breaking skin. Combine cooked potatoes with milk, butter, cheese, salt and pepper. Mash. Reserve for filling fried skins or use separately. When light goes out place skins in oil and deep-fry 8 to 10 minutes or until golden brown and crisp. Drain on tempura rack or absorbent paper towels. Fill with potato mixture or just sprinkle with salt. Fried skins sprinkled with salt or topped with sour cream are a delicious hors d'oeuvre.

Makes: 6 servings

Candied Carrots

Preparation time: 10 minutes
Cooking time: 20 minutes
Cooking technique: Steaming

½ cup water
1½ pounds carrots, peeled, cut in
    ¼-inch thick slices
1 tablespoon butter
2 tablespoons maple syrup

½ cup brown sugar, firmly packed
½ teaspoon cinnamon
½ teaspoon salt
1 tablespoon cornstarch

Place steamer insert or rack into wok. Pour water into wok. Place carrots on steamer insert. Set heat control dial at 250° F. Cover. Steam for 8 minutes or until tender-crisp. While carrots are steaming combine remaining ingredients. Remove carrots and steamer insert. Discard water. Return carrots to wok. Add remaining ingredients. Stir well to combine. Cook uncovered, stirring occasionally, until carrots are tender and sauce is thickened, about 10 minutes.

Makes: 8 servings

Potato Rice Croquettes

Preparation time: 20 minutes
Cooking time: 10 minutes
Cooking technique: Deep-frying

1½ cups cooked rice
3 boiled potatoes, mashed
3 tablespoons Parmesan cheese, grated
2 teaspoons salt

⅛ teaspoon pepper
1 egg
½ cup flavored dried bread crumbs

Set heat control dial at 425° F. While oil is heating, combine all ingredients except bread crumbs. Form mixture into 10 (3-inch) oval croquettes. Roll in flavored bread crumbs. When light goes out deep-fry for 8 to 10 minutes or until well browned. Drain on tempura rack or absorbent paper towels. Serve as an accompaniment to meat or fish.

Makes: 10

Steamed Rice

Preparation time: 2 minutes
Cooking time: 20 minutes
Cooking technique: Steaming

2½ cups water
1 cup rice
½ teaspoon salt

Pour water into wok. Set heat control dial at 225° F. When light goes out add rice and salt. Stir. Cover. Steam for 20 minutes or until water evaporates and rice is tender.

Makes: 3½ cups rice

Eggplant *Lasagna*

Preparation time: 15 minutes
Cooking time: 50 minutes
Cooking technique: Shallow-frying, Simmering

½ to ¾ cup vegetable oil
1 eggplant, (1 to 1½ pounds) cut
in slices
½ cup all-purpose flour
1 pound ricotta cheese
1 egg
¼ cup milk

1 teaspoon salt
¼ teaspoon pepper
¼ teaspoon dried basil
¼ teaspoon dried parsley
¼ cup grated Parmesan cheese
½ pound mozzerella cheese, grated
3 cups tomato sauce

Pour ½ cup vegetable oil into wok. Set heat control dial at 350° F. Dredge eggplant in flour, shaking off excess. When light goes out add 4 slices of eggplant to wok and shallow-fry until lightly browned, about 2 to 3 minutes per side. Drain on absorbent paper towels. Repeat until all eggplant is fried, adding oil as needed. While eggplant is frying combine ricotta, egg, milk, spices and 2 tablespoons of Parmesan cheese in a large bowl. Remove any remaining oil from wok after frying eggplant and wipe wok clean. Pour ½ cup tomato sauce into wok. Turn heat control dial to 225° F. Place ⅓ of the eggplant over sauce to cover bottom surface of wok. Spoon about ⅓ of the ricotta mixture over eggplant and top with ½ cup of the tomato sauce. Sprinkle with ⅓ of the remaining Parmesan cheese and ⅓ of the grated mozzerella. Continue to layer in the same manner ending with cheeses. Cover. Simmer until hot, about 30 minutes.

Makes: 6 servings

Fettucini Primavera

Preparation time: 10 minutes
Cooking time: 15 minutes
Cooking technique: Sautéeing

1 pound fettucini noodles
2 tablespoons butter or margarine
2 tablespoons olive oil
1 small onion, chopped
1 clove garlic, minced

1 medium zucchini, diced
¼ pound mushrooms, sliced
1 cup heavy cream
⅓ cup Parmesan cheese, grated
¼ teaspoon pepper

Cook fettucini according to package directions. While fettucini is cooking combine butter and oil in wok. Set heat control dial to 350° F. When butter begins to melt (do not wait for light to go out) add onions and garlic. Sauté until transparent, about 1 minute. When light goes out add zucchini and sauté until lightly browned, 3 to 5 minutes. Add mushrooms and sauté 1 minute. Pour cream, cheese and pepper over vegetables in wok. Stir well to combine and heat for 30 seconds. Add drained, cooked fettucini and toss to coat. Turn heat control to "off." Serve immediately directly from the wok or in a serving dish.

Makes: 4 to 6 servings

Ratatouille

Preparation time: 20 minutes
Cooking time: 20 minutes
Cooking technique: Sautéeing

½ cup vegetable oil
3 large cloves garlic, crushed
2 large onions, sliced
2 medium green peppers, cut in strips
2 large zucchini, unpeeled and sliced
1 pound eggplant, peeled and cubed

½ pound mushrooms, sliced
2 dozen cherry tomatoes, halved
3 tablespoons white wine
2 teaspoons salt
1 teaspoon Italian seasoning

Pour ¼ cup oil into wok. Set heat control dial at 350° F. When light goes out add garlic and onions and sauté until lightly browned, about 2 minutes. Push up sides of wok. Add remaining oil. When light goes out add green peppers and zucchini and sauté 5 minutes or until tender. Remove and reserve. Add eggplant and sauté 3 minutes. Remove and reserve. Add mushrooms and sauté 2 minutes. Return all vegetables to wok. Add remaining ingredients, stirring well to combine. Simmer, stirring occasionally, for 3 minutes.

Makes: 8 servings

Marinated Mushrooms and Cauliflower

Preparation time: 10 minutes
Cooking time: 10 minutes
Marinating time: 1 to 3 days
Cooking technique: Simmering

1 onion, finely chopped
2 cloves garlic, minced
1 teaspoon salt
¼ teaspoon pepper
2 teaspoon chopped parsley

¼ cup vegetable oil
1½ cups vinegar
⅛ to ¼ teaspoon thyme
¼ teaspoon basil
½ cup sugar

1 pound whole mushrooms, cleaned
1 small head cauliflower (1½ pounds)
  cut into florets

Place all ingredients except mushrooms and cauliflower into wok. Set heat control dial at 250° F. Bring mixture to a boil and continue to boil for 20 minutes. Place mushrooms and cauliflower into a large bowl. Pour pickling mixture over all. Allow to cool. Cover and refrigerate for at least 24 hours. Serve in salads or as an hors d'oeuvre.

Makes: about 2 quarts

Desserts

Steamed Rice Pudding

Preparation time: 5 minutes
Cooking time: 2 hours 15 minutes
Cooking technique: Steaming

5 cups water	½ cup sugar
2½ cups milk	¼ cup raisins
1 cup long grain rice, raw	1½ teaspoon vanilla extract

Place steamer insert or rack in wok. Pour water into wok. In a 1½-quart oven-proof casserole dish combine milk, rice, sugar and raisins. Place cassserole dish on steamer insert. Cover top of dish with waxed paper. Cover wok. Set heat control dial at 250° F. Steam for 2 to 2¼ hours. Stir pudding every 30 minutes. Check water level in wok every 30 minutes. Add water as needed, be sure not to let wok cook dry. During last 15 minutes stir in the vanilla extract. Serve warm or cold with whipped cream.

Makes: 6 servings

Custard Bread Pudding

Preparation time: 10 minutes
Cooking time: 1 hour
Cooking technique: Steaming

5 cups water	1 tablespoon vanilla extract
2 eggs	Pieces of stale bread cut into
½ cup sugar	cubes (about 8 cups)
1 quart milk	⅓ cup raisins
1 teaspoon cinnamon	

Place steamer insert or rack into wok. Pour water into wok. In a large mixing bowl combine eggs, sugar, milk, cinnamon and vanilla extract. Pour ⅓ of mixture into the bottom of a 1½-quart oven-proof casserole dish. Add ⅓ of the bread and raisins. Press down until bread absorbs some liquid. Continue to layer ingredients ending with milk mixture. Press down until bread absorbs most of the liquid. Place casserole dish on steamer insert, cover top of dish with waxed paper. Cover wok. Set heat control dial at 250° F. Steam. Check water level in wok after 30 minutes. Add water as needed, be sure not to let wok cook dry. Steam for an hour or until a knife inserted 1-inch from the center comes out dry. Serve warm or cold with whipped cream or ice cream.

Makes: 8 servings

Cakes and Donuts

Funnel Cakes

Preparation time: 5 minutes
Cooking time: 45 minutes
Cooking technique: Deep-frying

3 cups vegetable oil
2 cups all-purpose flour
¼ cup sugar
2 teaspoons baking powder
1 teaspoon salt
½ teaspoon cinnamon

1 teaspoon vanilla extract
¼ cup vegetable oil
1¾ cups milk
1 egg
confectioners' sugar

Pour oil into wok. Set heat control dial at 425° F. In a large bowl combine all ingredients except confectioners' sugar. When light goes out pour ¼ cup batter through a funnel into oil in a steady stream making a lacework-style pattern. Do 2 or 3 cakes at a time and fry until golden brown. Turn and brown on the other side. Drain on tempura rack or absorbent paper towels. Sprinkle with confectioners' sugar.

Makes: about 3 dozen (3-inch) cakes

Donuts

Preparation time: 2 hours 10 minutes
Cooking time: 15 minutes
Cooking technique: Deep-frying

2 packages (¼ ounce each) active
   dry yeast
¼ cup warm water
Pinch of sugar
1½ cups milk
⅓ cup melted butter
¼ cup sugar

2 teaspoons salt
½ teaspoon cinnamon
2 eggs, well beaten
1 teaspoon vanilla extract
5½ cups all-purpose flour
confectioners' sugar

In a small bowl dissolve yeast in warm water. Stir in a pinch of sugar. Allow mixture to stand in a warm, draft free place until yeast begins to bubble and grow, about 5 minutes. If it does not the yeast is dead. Start again. While yeast is growing pour milk into a saucepan and scald. Stir in butter, sugar, salt, cinnamon, eggs and vanilla extract. Cool to lukewarm. Stir yeast mixture into milk mixture and gradually add flour until dough forms a soft ball. Cover with a clean towel and set in a warm place to rise until doubled in bulk, about 45 minutes. Roll out to ¼-inch thick on a well-floured board. Cut with a floured donut cutter. Place donuts 1-inch apart on a lightly floured cookie sheet. Cover with towel and allow to rise until doubled in bulk, about 45 minutes. Pour oil into wok and set heat control dial at 425° F. When light goes out add donuts about 6 at a time and deep-fry until golden brown, about 1½ to 2 minutes per side. Continue until all donuts are fried. Fry donut holes. Sprinkle warm donuts with confectioners' sugar and serve while warm.

Makes: 24

Candies

Walnut Toffee

Preparation time: 5 minutes
Cooking time: 15 minutes
Cooking technique: Candy-making

½ pound butter or margarine
1⅔ cups sugar
1 tablespoon light corn syrup
¼ cup water

1½ cups coarsely chopped walnuts
2 bars (4 ounces each) German
   chocolate, melted
½ cup finely chopped walnuts

Measure all ingredients. Butter a 15½ x 10½ x 2-inch jelly roll pan. Reserve. Place butter, sugar, corn syrup and water into wok. Set heat control dial at 400° F. Begin stirring immediately. Stir constantly. When light goes out drop a small amount of candy off a spoon into cold water. If candy becomes hard and brittle turn heat control dial to "off." If it does not, raise temperature to 425° F., stirring constantly. Retest. Turn heat control to "off". Stir in coarsely chopped nuts and pour out onto prepared pan. Refrigerate until cooled, about 2 hours. While candy is cooling clean wok by filling it half full with water. Bring water to a rolling boil and then rinse. Turn heat control dial to 150° F. Add chocolate to wok. Melt chocolate. When candy is cooled, spread melted chocolate on top and sprinkle with finely chopped nuts. Refrigerate until chocolate hardens. Break into bite-size pieces.

Makes: about 1¾ pounds

Sweet and Salty Nut Clusters

Preparation time: 5 minutes
Cooking time: 15 minutes
Cooking technique: Candy-making

1 cup sugar
¼ cup butter or margaine
1 tablespoon vanilla extract

1 cup whole almonds, shelled
1 cup walnut halves, shelled
Salt

Measure all ingredients. Pour sugar and butter into wok. Set heat control dial at 350° F. Begin stirring immediately. Stir constantly until light goes out. When light goes out add vanilla extract and nuts. Stir constantly until sugar melts to a liquid stage, about 10 minutes. Drop candy by heaping tablespoonsful onto aluminum foil. Sprinkle with salt. Cool.

Makes: about 1 pound

Note: For easy cleanup, fill wok half full with water, bring to a rolling boil and then rinse.

Rocky Road

Preparation time: 5 minutes
Cooking time: 5 minutes
Cooking technique: Candy-making

1 package (12 ounces) semi-sweet
   chocolate morsels
2 tablespoons milk
2 tablespoons butter

3 cups miniature marshmallows
¾ cup broken walnuts, shelled
1 teaspoon vanilla extract

Measure all ingredients. Butter an 8 x 8 x 2-inch square pan. Reserve. Place chocolate morsels, milk and butter into wok. Set heat control dial at 350° F. Begin stirring immediately. Stir constantly until chocolate is melted and milk and butter are incorporated. Stir in remaining ingredients. Turn heat control dial to "off." Spread mixture into prepared pan. Refrigerate until firm, about 2 hours.

Makes: 64 (1-inch) pieces

Note: For easy cleanup, fill wok half full with water, bring to a rolling boil and then rinse.

Chocolate Almond Breakup

Preparation time: 5 minutes
Cooking time: 10 minutes
Cooking technique: Candy-making

2 cups sugar
3 tablespoons butter or margarine
½ teaspoon salt
¾ cup evaporated milk

8 squares (1 ounce each) semi-sweet
   chocolate
¾ cup almonds, shelled and chopped
1 teaspoon vanilla extract

Measure all ingredients. Butter an 8 x 8 x 2-inch pan. Reserve. Place sugar, butter, salt and milk into wok. Set heat control dial at 350° F. Bring mixture to a boil, stirring constantly. Allow mixture to boil for 3 minutes. Turn heat control dial to "off." Add remaining ingredients. Stir just until combined. Pour into buttered pan immediately. Refrigerate until firm, about 2 hours.

Makes: 64 (1-inch) pieces

Note: For easy cleanup, fill wok half full with water, bring to a rolling boil and then rinse.

Crêpes and Omelets

Basic Crêpes

Preparation time: 5 minutes
Cooking time: 40 minutes
Cooking technique: Crêpe-making

2 eggs, well beaten
1 cup all-purpose flour
1 cup milk

2 tablespoons vegetable oil
1 teaspoon salt

In a large bowl combine all ingredients. Mix well with a wire whisk to remove all lumps. Set heat control dial at 325° F. When light goes out dip a paper towel in vegetable oil and wipe bottom surface of wok with the towel. Pour 3 tablespoons of batter into wok. Tilt wok to completely cover the bottom of wok with batter. Cook until crêpe is browned on first side, about 2 minutes. Turn and cook until browned, about 2 minutes. Remove to plate. Place waxed paper between crêpes as they are cooked. Use in any recipe calling for crêpes. Crêpes can be frozen for future use.

Makes: 10 crêpes

Mushroom Cheese Omelet

Preparation time: 5 minutes
Cooking time: 5 minutes
Cooking technique: Sautéeing, Shallow-frying

2 tablespoons butter
1 small onion, minced
6 mushrooms, sliced
3 eggs, well beaten

½ teaspoon salt
Pinch of pepper
1 slice cheese, broken in pieces

Place 1 tablespoon butter into wok. Set heat control dial at 300° F. When butter melts (do not wait for light to go out) add onions and sauté until lightly browned, about 1 minute. Add mushrooms and sauté 30 seconds. Push up sides of wok. Add remaining butter. When butter melts add eggs, salt and pepper. Allow eggs to set, do not stir. When eggs begin to set, lift up sides of omelet and allow egg mixture to slide under. When eggs are almost set add cheese. When cheese melts fold omelet in half and serve immediately.

Makes: 1 large omelet

Substitutions: Add cooked meats or your favorite vegetables with onions and cook as above.

Do-ahead Brunch *Crêpes*

Preparation time: 5 minutes
Cooking time: 50 minutes
Cooking technique: Crêpe-making, Steaming

FILLING MIXTURE:

¾ pound breakfast sausage meat
1 medium onion, chopped
1 clove garlic, minced
2 cups spinach, cleaned and
  finely chopped

1 egg, well beaten
3 ounces cream cheese
2 tablespoons grated Parmesan
  cheese

1 recipe Basic Crêpes (page 133)

SAUCE MIXTURE:

2 tablespoons butter or margarine
2 tablespoons all-purpose flour
2 cups milk
3 cups water

¼ cup grated Cheddar cheese
2 tablespoons white wine

Set heat control dial at 300° F. Add sausage, onions and garlic. Do not wait for light to go out; sauté until sausage is well browned, about 8 minutes. While sausage is browning, combine remaining filling ingredients. Add to wok. Stir well to combine. Remove and reserve. Wash wok. Make crêpes according to directions for Basic Crêpes on page 133.

To make sauce: Place butter into wok. Set heat control dial at 250° F. When butter begins to melt (do not wait for light to go out), stir in flour to form a paste. Add milk, stirring well until sauce thickens. Add cheese and wine and stir well to combine. Turn heat control dial to "off." Stir ¼ cup of sauce into filling mixture. Place about ¼ cup of filling mixture in the center of each crêpe and roll. Pour half of the sauce into a 9-inch square cake pan or 1-quart oblong baking dish. Place crêpes, seam-side-down into pan. Pour remaining sauce over crêpes. Cover pan with foil and refrigerate until 1½ hours before serving time. Pour water into wok. Place steamer insert or rack into wok. Set heat control dial at 250° F. Place covered baking dish on insert and heat for 30 minutes or until hot. Serve directly from wok or remove to serving platter.

Makes: 4 to 6 servings

Next-day *Manicotti Crêpes*

Preparation time: 20 minutes
Cooking time: 30 minutes
Cooking technique: Crêpe-making, Steaming

FILLING
1 pound ricotta cheese
3 tablespoons grated Parmesan
cheese
1 egg
⅓ pound mozzarella cheese, grated

¼ teaspoon salt
⅛ teaspoon pepper
2 teaspoons chopped parsley
¼ cup milk

10 crêpes (recipe on page 133)
2½ cups Tomato Sauce (page 123)
3 cups water

In a large bowl combine filling mixture. Spread about ¼ cup filling into center of each crêpe. Roll. Fill all crêpes in the same manner. Pour 1¼ cups tomato sauce into bottom of a 9-inch square cake pan or a 1-quart oblong baking dish. Place crêpes seam-side-down into dish. Cover with remaining sauce. Cover dish with foil and refrigerate until 1½ hours before serving time.

Pour water into wok. Place steamer insert or rack into wok. Set heat control dial at 250° F. Place covered dish on rack. Cover wok. Heat for 30 minutes or until hot. Sprinkle with additional cheese and serve.

Makes: 4 to 6 servings

Crêpes Suzettes

Preparation time: 20 minutes
Cooking time: 25 minutes
Cooking technique: Crêpe-making,

¼ cup butter or margarine
½ cup brown sugar
¼ cup orange juice
¼ cup Amaretto liquer

1 tablespoon cognac
1 recipe of Basic Crêpes
⅛ teaspoon cinnamon
2 teaspoons sugar

Place butter in wok. Set heat contol dial at 300° F. When butter begins to melt, (do not wait for light to go out) add remaining ingredients except crêpes, cinnamon and sugar. Simmer, stirring constantly just until sugar melts and butter is incorporated, about 2 minutes. Combine cinnamon and sugar. Dip crêpes into sauce and sprinkle with cinnamon and sugar. Fold crêpes in quarters. Arrange crêpes on platter, pour sauce over all. Serve immediately.

Makes: 4 to 6 servings

Dessert *Blintzes*

Preparation time: 10 minutes
Cooking time: 30 minutes
Cooking technique: Crêpe-making, Shallow-frying

CREPES:
4 eggs, lightly beaten
1 cup water
⅓ cup milk

3 tablespoons melted butter or
    margarine
1 cup all-purpose flour
¾ teaspoon salt

1 recipe Cheese Filling
2 tablespoons butter or margarine

1 cup sour cream, or whipped cream
1 can (21 ounces) prepared cherry,
    blueberry or apple pie filling

In a large bowl combine eggs, water, milk and butter. Add flour and salt to egg mixture. Stir until smooth. Set heat control dial at 325° F. When light goes out, dip a paper towel into vegetable oil and wipe the bottom surface of wok with the towel. Pour 3 tablespoons batter into wok. Tilt wok to completely cover the bottom with batter. Cook until top is dry and bottom is lightly browned. Do not turn. Remove. Repeat until all pancakes are made. Prepare Cheese Filling by combining all ingredients.

CHEESE FILLING:
2 cups (1 pound) cream-style cottage
    cheese
1 egg, slightly beaten
2 tablespoons melted butter or
    margarine

3 tablespoons sugar
½ teaspoon ground cinnamon
¼ teaspoon salt

Place 2 tablespoons cheese filling on the browned side of each pancake. Lift one edge of crêpe and fold to center. Fold opposite side to overlap. Tuck in ends to form a rectangle. Just before serving, place 1 tablespoon butter into wok. Set heat control dial at 275° F. When butter melts (do not wait until light goes out) place 4 or 5 blintzes into wok. Fry until lightly browned on both sides, about 3 to 4 minutes per side. Add remaining butter and fry remaining blintzes. Serve hot, topped with sour cream or whipped cream and fruit filling.

Makes: 12

Glossary of Oriental Ingredients

Baby corn: Miniature ears of corn about 2½-inches long, sold in jars.

Bean curd: *(Tofu)* Made from soy beans. Soft, smooth and bland, but takes on the flavor of soups and sauces to which it is added. High in protein.

Bean sauce: Residue left after soy sauce is manufactured. A thick paste used to flavor pork or poultry.

Bean sprouts: Mung bean sprout. Crispy in texture, can be eaten raw or cooked.

Bird's nest: Nest of sea swallow. Made by the action of the saliva of the bird with the bits of fish with which he makes his nest. A gelatinous and strawy mass, must be cleaned and soaked before use. Considered a rare delicacy.

Black beans: Tiny, soft and very salty bean. Used as a seasoning for meats and seafood.

Bok Choy: A leafy green vegetable which looks like swiss chard. Mild in flavor.

Cellophane noodles: Very thin noodles made from ground mung beans. Break into small pieces before soaking since they stick together after cooking. Should be soaked before use in soup. They can also be deep-fried and used as an accompaniment to stir-fried dishes.

Chinese parsley: Also known as the herb coriander. Used as a garnish or as a bouquet in roasting poultry.

Chinese cabbage: Tall tightly packed vegetable which is milder than cabbage. Used in soups or stir-fried foods.

Chinese sausage: Pork sausages which are usually sliced thin before use. Used in many different types of dishes.

Chili oil: Red chili pepper flavored oil.

Chutney: Sauce made from peaches and apricots. Used as a condiment

Cloud ear fungus: A blend of star anise, cinnamon, cloves, fennel and anise pepper.

Ginger, sweet mixed: (sub gum vegetables) Sweet and sour ginger mixed with vegetables. Use as a garnish or a relish.

Glutinous rice: Short round shaped rice, very sticky when cooked.

Glutinous rice flour: Flour milled from glutinous rice.

Hoisin sauce: Deep brownish red sauce made from soy beans, chili, garlic and vinegar. Has a spicy sweet flavor.

Lemon sauce: Sauce made from lemon and sugar. Used to season duck or used as a jam.

Lichee: A red fruit which looks like a round strawberry. Sweet. Available in cans.

Lilybuds: Dried buds of the tiger lily. Must be soaked prior to use. Before soaking knot to prevent falling apart. Small lump at the end of each should be removed.

Mushrooms, dried Chinese: Must be soaked prior to use. Stems are discarded, use caps only.

Mustard greens: Green leafy vegetable which is somewhat bitter. Used in soups or it can be pickled.

Oyster sauce: Thick brown sauce made from oysters, but there is no strong fishy odor. Used as a condiment or as a seasoning for meat.

Plum sauce: Sauce made from plums, apricots, vinegar and sugar. Similar to chutney and used as a condiment.

Red dates, dried: (jujube nuts)Dried red fruits which are used in soups and steamed dishes to add sweetness.

Rice noodles: Soft, flat noodles made from rice flour.

Salted eggs: Duck eggs which have been soaked in brine at least 40 days. Cook and use like a hard-boiled egg.

Sesame oil: A seasoning oil with a nut-like flavor which is sprinkled on top of prepared foods for flavoring.

Soy sauce: Sauce made from soy beans, wheat, yeast and salt. There are two kinds, the light and thin and the heavy and black variety. Both are used as condiments. Can be very salty.

Star anise: A cluster of dark brown dry seeds shaped like a flower and has a licorice flavor.

Straw mushrooms: Fragile and delicate, used to flavor seafood or vegetable dishes.

Sweet bean paste: A puree of red beans used as a filling for Chinese pastries.

Tapioca starch: Used as a sauce thickener and for making wrappers for some Chinese pastries.

Taro: Root of a tropical plant similar to a potato but more delicate in flavor.

Tea melon: (sweet cucumber) A squash preserved in honey and spices. Used as a condiment or steamed in pork dishes.

Tofu: See Bean cake.

Water chestnuts: Chestnuts grown in water and resembling ordinary chestnuts before peeling. White and crunchy with a sweet flavor. Readily available in cans.

Glossary of Oriental Ingredients

RECIPE INDEX

pork roast, 26
pork Szechuan, 62

V

Veal, in Swedish meatballs, 106
Vegetable(s),
  and beef *pizziola*, 114
  beer-batter dipped, 112
  candied carrots, 125
  cauliflower,
    with cheese sauce, 124
    with crabmeat sauce, 71
  chicken and, 80
  corn, miniature, and straw
    mushrooms, 54
  deep-fried potato skins, 125
  eggplant,
    lasagna, 127
    spicy, 61
    stuffed, Korean, 90
  fettucini primavera, 127

fritters, Korean, 89
Japanese cabbage rolls, 80
marinated mushrooms and cauliflower, 128
potato, ham and egg hash, 115
potato-rice croquettes, 126
ratatouille, 128
rice,
  and beans, Korean, 91
  fried *sub gum*, 69
  potato croquettes, 126
  Spanish, 121
  steamed, 126
stir-fry, 36
stuffed mushrooms, 75
with *tofu*, 57

W

Walnut toffee, 131
Water chestnuts, 138
Wontons, fried, 40, 41

Recipe Index